A DARK PAST

~ a selection of Rhondda murders ~

by

Elaine Hawkins

and

Avril Evans

First published 2002
Reprinted 2003

Published by Whitchurch Books Ltd.
67 Merthyr Road, Whitchurch,
Cardiff CF14 1DD

ISBN 0 9539771 1 0

Printed by J & P Davison
3 James Place, Treforest, Pontypridd, Mid Glamorgan CF37 1SQ

ACKNOWLEDGMENTS

The authors wish to thank those who helped in contributing to the writing of this book, without whom, this book may not have been possible.

Many thanks to Nick Kelland, librarian in the reference section of Treorchy Library.

Thanks to Ken Williams and Dave Owen (Maerdy Archives) for the enthusiastic support given during the writing of this book, especially to Ken who helped in providing research material and expressed good wishes in hoping that this work be a success.

A special thanks to Eddie Wilde and Sylvia Wilde, relatives of Ethel Adlam, for their willingness to help provide details of Ethel's life and tragic demise.

Our thanks to all whose names may not have been mentioned, thank you for all of your support.

Avril and Elaine

CONTENTS

LIST OF ILLUSTRATIONS

INTRODUCTION

The dictionary definition of murder is the 'unlawful, premeditated killing of a human being.'

Unlawful those killings may be, but I don't think that the majority were premeditated. A person's actions are often guided by the unforeseen circumstances or outside influences that arise and the result can be murder.

Alcohol is one influence that can heighten the passions of a normally calm individual and push them into actions that are as a rule alien to them. There is definite proof that there is a direct link between violent crime and alcohol. This link was recognised in the 19th and 20th centuries, although the 20th century has seen drug abuse as having a more definite role in violent crime.

Another influence is the stress caused by extreme poverty and uncertainty, but at the end of the day we cannot put the entire blame on outside influences and unforeseen circumstances as we are all ultimately responsible for our own actions and we must bear the responsibility and cost when those actions are unlawful.

When investigating the murders of the 19th and 20th centuries our first source was to look through the local papers, where, as well as giving contemporary reports, it was also interesting to note the differences in the way that the murders were reported in the earlier years as opposed to the way we report them now. The early reports were very melodramatic and Victorian; instead of printing just the facts, the reports were impregnated with early 20th century values and prejudices and with clear racial discrimination. There are also clear differences between 19th and 20th century definitions of crimes. Many activities that were deemed as criminal in the 19th century, e.g. suicide, are now no longer recognised as crimes in the 20th century. This does not mean that the crime rate has dropped but that the types of crime have changed.

Modernisation in the 20th century has seen the introduction of major drug abuse, computer crimes, organised crimes and auto crime. The cost of crime is now far higher. The 19th century crimes were of a more petty nature and a 'criminal class' was not recognised; a small group of people committed all the crimes. Then as today, most criminals were young, male and working class. But murder has always in both centuries been viewed as a serious crime.

It is tempting to look back at 19th century Wales and see it as a dark and violent time, particularly in the South with its industrialism, i's mines, poor housing, overcrowding and poverty. Although it is true that the crime rate was higher in the urban areas than it was in the rural ones, violent crime was lower in Wales than in any other country in Great Britain in the 19th century.

A quote from the ' Rhondda Leader' of the 5th January 1901, which was a reflection on a new millennium, bears this out when it states, '........ the history of the Rhondda in crime has not the dark picture that many outside the valleys would have us believe. Nothing very serious has been recorded and the worst of them can, without any extreme, be classed as the usual petty offences..

.. Candidly we claim for the Rhondda in 1900, and we know it pretty well, an indication positive of better attitude and a more sensible view of recreation.' I think that this says a lot for the people of South Wales when they were going through a particularly turbulent and changeable time in history, with the impact and speed at which the industrial revolution was changing and affecting their lives.

Statistically then, the incidence of murder was low in the 19th and early 20th centuries. There were on average only twenty cases of homicide a year between 1834 and 1900, with manslaughter being five times as common. Also interesting was that about half the cases were family affairs and even in cases outside the family, the parties concerned usually knew each other intimately. The accused were usually male, but in the rare cases where women were the guilty party the victims were often children, usually under the age of one; women rarely murdered adults.

Although the murder rate was low in Wales, a perusal of the local papers printed in the early 19th century showed that working class society was often a violent and cruel place to live. The instances of murder might be few, but the instances of drunkenness, wife-beating , child neglect and cruelty to animals were practically weekly occurrences. The crimes were also an indication of the poverty of working class families and the hardships and difficulties they faced with drink, drunkenness being a manifestation of their troubled lives.

Towards the end of the 19th century and the early part of the 20th century, the crime rate dropped as social attitudes changed. This change was due to better education, better policing, night schools, temperance societies and religious revivals.

Society became more civilised and adopted higher moral standards and was less tolerant of crime, but since the 1950s, the crime rate has again started to climb and violent crimes especially, often linked to drug abuse, are on the increase.

However, it is the crime of murder that stands out from all the other crimes and produces the deepest feelings and the keenest interest amongst the public. Murders, along with arson, are the only two crimes to cover such a wide range of motives and emotions. From the cold calculating planned murder to the psychopathic frenzy of the insane, it is the taking of another life prematurely and violently that cuts deepest into the core of our susceptibilities and understanding.

Unlike other crimes that showed noticeable differences in different centuries, the numbers of murders and the manner of violent deaths has changed little over the years and murderers themselves were unlike other offenders. Perhaps it is this timeless quality that sends a chill to the bone, the idea that despite changing attitudes, new laws and legislation, better policing, there will always be someone willing and able to take another person's life.

The crime of murder therefore raises many questions and although we can try and view a case objectively to see the barest facts, it is perhaps impossible to divorce this from the subjective view. It is perhaps impossible to remain detached and unfeeling, not to see beyond the facts to the feelings and often shattered lives of those families, both the victims and the accused, that have been damaged irreparably by the tragic event.

The most difficult question a murder raises is also the simplest and also the unanswerable one of WHY?.

We hope in the following pages to try to go some way to answering this question. For although the cases concerned, then caused shock and disbelief, with the detachment of time and in retrospect this task would now seem an easier one.

Finally our purpose in writing this book was to construct a historical document and investigate the attitudes and policing methods that existed then as compared to today. It proves overall, we feel, that although Wales was often depicted as a place with many black spots of deprivation and crime, it is a place where certainly the crime of murder is still rare and remains statistically lower than in the rest of the UK as was the case in times past.

Avril Evans

During the course of history so many aspects of our lives, indeed of our world, have changed. A lot has improved for us, with advancements in technology and medicine we have better standards of living and better working conditions. We have transport, gas, electricity and good sanitation, which in itself eliminates a lot of diseases like typhoid that our ancestors had to live with. We have opportunities that our ancestors could only in their wildest dreams have hoped to see and experience. In fact our lives today, along with our standards of living, we owe to those who walked before us. It was through their hardships and determination born from those hardships, that the pioneers stood forward and fought for the changes that gave inspiration to others in moving our society forwards to what it is today.

Yet despite all of our changes one thing has not changed at all, human nature. For as long as history has dictated, amongst the good, the brave and figures that we admire, respect and revere as heroes, lurk those who reflect the dark side of man's nature. History still hands down to us hearts full of greed, lust and hatred, creating the infamous killers that we know today.

It is with a morbid fascination that we recall these crimes and wish to know the details of the poor victims' grisly yet untimely end. I say poor victims lest we do forget them, as we must remember that for every murder, indeed for every crime committed, there are victims.

Whether it be the poor soul whose life has been cruelly snuffed out, or the families who suffer the burdens of their losses, there are victims.

The question here arises, why do we always seem to be so fascinated with just the killers and the criminals, wanting to know about their past and what it is that lays within that past, which may or may not point to what led to the creation of the monsters that they have become? Is it because a part of us almost fears the fact that given a certain set of circumstances we ourselves could lose control and become one of the monsters that we so much love to hate by committing the ultimate crime against our own kind?

Whatever it is that attracts us to those who often remind us of the dark dangerous side of our own nature, we must remember the victims and hope that we ourselves won't be included in that long list of names that grows. The victims had lives and families, their lives and families' lives must be viewed and given the compassion that they deserve.

In today's society, population levels are high, crime is more commonplace and murder, still a rare crime to be committed in South Wales, is today more commonplace than it was in years gone by. With vastly improved systems of communication with the outside world, via television, radio and satellite, we constantly are being fed with news of murders and atrocities of the most terrible nature that frequently occur in various locations around the world. Yet it is only the mass murders or particularly vicious killings that seem to capture the imagination and sympathy of the press and public alike. Do we temporarily stop becoming complacent about crime and cry out our protests, showing our shock, horror and grief only when a child is killed or a mass murder is committed?

The tragedy of Dunblane is still and always will be remembered. Many a mother shed a tear on that day in man's chillingly dark history. The moors murders are still much publicised to this day.

The Fred and Rose West murders and also Dr Harold Shipman, will be for ever referred to and left unforgotten. Wales, thank God has so far been spared the shame of serial killers.

We should remember more the victims than their killers. Each life snuffed out is a tragedy in itself, causing suffering and agonising grief for those who knew the victim. Are we so hard and uncaring today that it takes a mass murder to wake us up to what seems to be becoming a more common crime? Perhaps fear again raises its ugly head, as we secretly think to ourselves, 'there but for the grace of God go I' and thank God that it happened to someone else and it was not us, who caught the ticket to the cemetery. How ignorant we can be in forgetting that if it can happen to the neighbour next door, it most certainly can happen to us.

In this book, we look at murders that have occurred in the Rhondda Valleys. Some are crimes of passion, some are of greed, some of the crimes may even be with no apparent motive other than that the killer 'lost his temper.' Whatever was in the killer's mind at the time of the killing, we hope that the reader will remember the victims also. It does not matter how long ago their life's story reached its conclusion, compassion must be held for the fact that families live on. The lives of the victim's future generations can and have been affected and influenced, positively and negatively.

I understand how the mind can ponder over relatives from the past who have been murdered, as during the 1700s my six times removed great grandmother and her son were murdered. They had a toll house in Guisely, Yorkshire, and it was for their toll money that they were murdered.

As a result of the double murder my five times removed great grandfather emigrated to Nova Scotia, hence this is where my American and Canadian roots were born. So here is a typical example of how future generations become affected. If the murders had not occurred then great, great .... grandpa may never have left Yorkshire. Amazingly enough history's events then led part of my family back to Britain culminating in my mother marrying a Welshman of many a generation. It is amazing though to think about how our family roots may have spread or who my mother could have been married to now, had those murders not been committed. My own family line, my heritage could be so different today. I might not even have existed if things had been different. It is these thoughts that brings me to the point. Future generations born after these events still feel the effect and are influenced by the crimes of the past, due to the lives of those people who altered their course of direction after being affected by the crime.

It is with these thoughts in mind that we would like to dedicate this book to the memories of the victims and their families in order that the world know of them and their lives and to acknowledge their existence and the importance their existence had for those who knew and loved them.

Elaine Hawkins

THE TYNTYLA FARM MURDER 1862

It must have been cold on the Sunday evening of December 2nd 1862 when in the fading light of an early winter's evening a brutal crime occurred.

Twenty-three year old Jane Lewis was, during that winter, staying as a guest of her aunt and uncle, Mr and Mrs Williams, at their home on Tyntyla Farm, deep in the Rhondda Valley.

On that fateful evening, Jane like other God fearing people in the valley, prepared herself against the chilly winter evening and left her aunt and uncles farmhouse in order to make her way to the Welsh Baptist chapel at Heolfach.

Walking briskly in order to keep warm, Jane Lewis decided to take a short cut to the chapel through the surrounding woodland. Her decision to do so was for Jane to be fatal.

Somewhere along the route of her journey, in the darkened lonely surrounding woodland, Jane met an unknown (even to this day) assailant, who with a savage ferocity cut her throat with such force that Jane was almost decapitated.

Strangely enough though, when the body of Jane Lewis was found, it was concluded at first that she had committed suicide. The idea of suicide was formed when, upon examination of her body, she was found to be pregnant. The conclusion of suicide was quickly denounced due to the severity of Jane's injuries. During enquiries that were subsequently made, it was discovered that Jane Lewis' throat had been cut with a razor, her uncle's razor in fact, which was usually kept in the farmhouse on the top of a grandfather clock.

Suspicion soon fell on Tom Williams, Jane's boyfriend. Tom Williams was known locally as 'Tom of the screens'. He was a man known by all to be 'sober industrious and respectable in all respects.' Despite his apparent good character, Tom was taken into custody by a Sergeant. Wise, but was released after making a statement. Tom's statement read, that although he and Jane had arranged to meet at the Baptist Chapel on the Sunday night at six o' clock, Jane had not turned up at the arranged time.

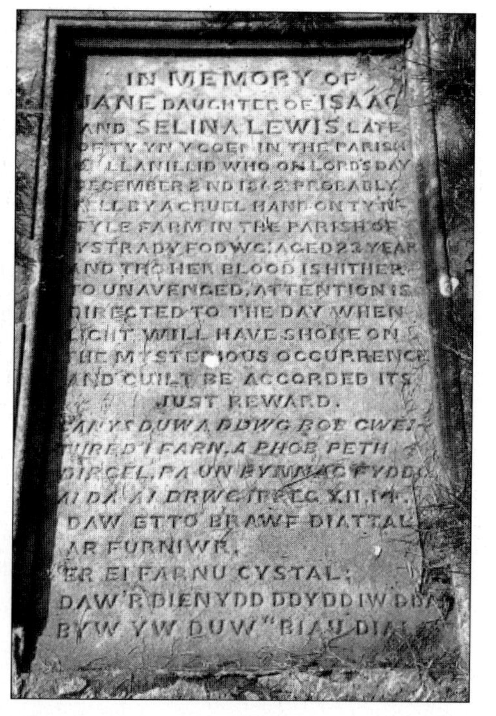

Photograph of stone laid in memory of the murder victim Jane Lewis.

Tom, apparently concerned by Jane's failure to meet him went to Tyntyla Farm to find out where she was. Strangely, Tom stated that he had not gone by the shortest route, which was through the woods, but via the longer route, which was up a slanting cart track.

The magistrates' investigation into the Jane Lewis murder took place in the long room at the New Inn Hotel in Pontypridd. It was here that the first verdict of suicide was announced, causing outrage amongst those who had been shocked and the death of such a young robust woman who by accounts was considered to be very attractive.

The Police, despite the coroner's verdict were sure it was murder and another suspect soon became the subject of Police interest. David Thomas, a farm labourer working on Tyntyla Farm who was also a relative of the dead girl and an unsuccessful suitor for her hand, was arrested and charged with her murder. This caused a sensation and a split in the surrounding communities, one half being in favour of the suicide theory, the other in favour of murder.

The magisterial investigation, held at the New Inn, lasted for several days. Mr Perkins was the presiding justice and Mr Stockwood prosecuted. The whole proceeding was watched by a public that was totally absorbed in interest over the whole matter.

David Thomas, the prisoner, was a 'short, stolid looking, grey eyed man, the type of an intellect running in the mechanical grooves of an

Ainon Memorial Park, Tonyrefail. Tyntyla Farm Murder, 1862

agricultural labourer.' The defence for David Thomas was a Mr Verity, a solicitor from Bridgend.

Despite being accused of murder, David Thomas betrayed no signs of emotion during the proceedings that were taking place. It was only on one occasion that the prisoner showed any change in expression, this being when under the dim light of candles, the bonnet worn by Jane Lewis was produced. The ribbons stained deeply with the blood of the dead girl caused the pallor of the prisoner to alter. Also produced was the razor that had been used to end Jane Lewis' life. The bloodstained razor still had a portion of the dead girl's thumb which had been sliced off in the attack on her adhered to it.

Mr. Verity fought vigorously in his defence for David Thomas, who was at that time committed for trial. However no damning evidence could be linked to David Thomas in connection to the murder and the grand jury threw out the bill.

David Thomas's return to the valley was 'hailed with vociferous acclamations' as many believed him to be innocent of the crime and had shown their support in subscribing to his defence.

Thomas Edmunds, a servant working at Tyntyla farm was also brought under suspicion and he too was arrested but released through lack of evidence.

The murderer of Jane Lewis was never caught and the victim of a heinous crime was buried at Ainon Baptist Chapel in Tonyrefail.

Shortly after her burial Tom Williams, Jane's lover and presumably the father of her unborn child, took lodgings in Tonyrefail, the lodgings being within a hundred yards of Jane's last resting place. He was by now a broken man and appeared to be 'on the verge of insanity.'

Tom stayed at the lodgings for only a short amount of time before emigrating to Australia.

About two years later, , near Ballarat in Australia, a Mr Richard Packer and his father were standing on the doorstep of their home, when they observed a strange man walking along the road hurling stones at the houses. He stopped when he saw the men and recognising them as Welshmen, he asked them if they had heard of the murder of Jane Lewis at Tyntyla Farm.

When the men replied in the affirmative, the man said, 'It was I that killed her.' With that he walked on, restarting his strange behaviour. After that day the man was never seen again.

If this man was Tom Williams and it seems likely that it was, it would appear that even after travelling to the other end of the world, he could not escape the memory of what he had done to Jane Lewis.

Jane Lewis was as stated buried at Ainon chapel; she was the first person to be buried in the churchyard, the chapel being under construction at the time.

The chapel has since been pulled down, today in its place stands a memorial park contained within a children's playground. The few gravestones at the site are placed in a narrow railed off area and Jane's gravestone lies flat on the ground next to the stone bearing the chapel's name.

The words on her gravestone translated from Welsh read; 'One day there will be unquestionable proof ; the murderer will be caught and will receive his trial. God is always alive, and always watching'

Such was the notoriety of the murder that its history lives on and Jane herself was immortalised in a fictional story by Isaac Craigfryn Hughes. The story was based on the facts of the murder and was called; The *TRAGEDY IN GELLI WOOD*. The small volume was published in 1909 and priced at 6d. A copy of the book can be seen in the Treorchy reference library. Since that time, the murder of Jane Lewis has been recalled in local newspaper articles and on the television, such is the interest that is still today generated from a vicious murder that forever will remain in the annals of criminal history as unsolved.

Appendix to the Tyntyla Farm Murder.

It is by today's standards without a doubt strange that the few suspects in the Tyntyla Farm murder were released and that no-one was convicted for the crime, Yet for the day, it is not too surprising at all. Details of the case are limited and the reader as well as the authors can only ponder on the many questions that arose as a result of Jane Lewis's death.

It is uncertain who it was that found the body of Jane Lewis and whether the razor used to kill her was left at the scene of the crime or put back in its place on the clock in the farmhouse.

Without even basic forensic science, catching the killer would have depended more upon a confession, a witness or sheer luck.

Jane Lewis met her fate in 1862, it was not until 1879 that criminology met its birth in the Police Headquarters of Paris. A policeman by the name of Alphonse Bertillon created the first form of filing system. This he did by measuring convicts, noting features and any distinguishing marks. It was not until around 1865-70 that a man called William Hershel invented the first form of fingerprinting and Sir Francis Galton devised a simple method of classifying and filing fingerprints. It was not until 1892-93 that fingerprinting was introduced as a scientific method of detection.

In 1900 came the discovery by Paul Uhlenhith of how to test blood to prove whether it was human or not. It was not until after the murder of Jane Lewis that a police force was properly created and forensic science became as we know it to be today. Sadly even the humble breakthroughs in crime detection came just a little too late for Jane Lewis.

THE CYMMER WIFE MURDER

Murders come under the category of being 'crimes of passion' when one partner, overwrought through jealousy and rage can turn from an ordinary hard working spouse and parent to a deranged, homicidal maniac. It leads one to speculate on what it is that occurs in the human brain to cause a person to suddenly behave insanely for a short period of time and then, immediately the deed is done, to go straight to the police in order to confess their crime, the period of insanity having dispersed as quickly as it arose. It is almost as if the more primitive part of our make-up takes over and passions overrule the more modern part of our grey matter. Such was the case on Friday 21st July 1893 in Cymmer, a small village on the outskirts of Porth.

The Pontypridd and District Herald of Saturday 22 July 1893 reported the case under the heading "Determined Murder of a Wife at Cymmer."

The article opened, rather like a Victorian novel, giving a prosaic description of the surrounding area where the persons involved in the drama lived. "About three miles and three quarters from Pontypridd, either by rail or by road, is situated the flourishing and busy town of Porth." The travel up the Cymmer hill to Trebanog was described as "....... an arduous task from the heat in summer and from the snows and frost of winter."

Nearby, at the top of the hill stood a small cluster of cottages called Rickards Row, with a pub, The Rickards Arms nearby. It was in one of these cottages that the Davies family lived. Edward Davies was described in the paper as a ".....quite stolid, hardworking collier" who was known to his friends, " ..as is the custom among miners as Ned Hezeiah."

Edward Davies, a twice married man was the father of ten children. He and his second wife who was not named in the case had six of the children from their union together, the children being four sons and two daughters. Although Davies had been described favourably by the paper and his friends, much doubt had been cast over the character of Mrs Davies. It had

Rickards Row

been reported that she was "devoted to the Salvation Army at Porth and spent most of her time attending its meetings, thus neglecting her own domestic duties." Rumours were also in circulation as to the familiar relations between Mrs Davies and the late Captain of the Army at Porth, which went so far as to assume that she was pregnant by him. These rumours soon fell upon the ears of Edward Davies, who received much 'chuffing' from his fellow workmates about his wife's behaviour.

All this was to greatly affect Edward Davies's peace of mind. But like the opening scenes of a tragedy in the theatre, the signs could only be recognised by those who had read the play.

So much was Edward affected by the rumours that early at 6.15 a.m.. on Friday 21st July 1893, he returned to his home, having been out to a neighbours house and sat down by the fireside.

His fifteen year old daughter Elizabeth Jane Davies, was making breakfast and had called Mrs Davies to see if she was getting up. Hearing the reply in the affirmative, Edward Davies arose from his chair without a word, reached for something in the cupboard and then proceeded up the stairs to the bedroom that his wife was in.

The sound of her mother screaming hysterically caused the young Elizabeth to run to the foot of the stairs, where to her horror she saw her father holding her mother by the head and drawing something across her throat. With blood now pouring from her neck Mrs Davies struggled to make her way down the stairs and out of the house where she managed to escape to her neighbour Mrs Flowers, who immediately gave her sanctuary in her home.

Edward Davies however was in hot pursuit of his wife Elizabeth his daughter followed closely behind trying to stop her father from catching up with her heavily bleeding injured mother.

Before Edward Davies could be stopped, he burst into Mrs. Flowers' house and grabbed his wife. Holding her head against the table Edward Davies slit his wife's throat for a second time.

The second wound proved to be a fatal wound. Mrs. Davies, supported by Mrs. Flowers who placed her on the chair next to the table, sat dying before her daughter's eyes.

Bravely Mrs. Flowers followed Edward Davies out of the house and confronted him outside.

Edward Davies said nothing, so Mrs. Flowers took him by his arm and led him to his own house.

At the house she told him "Now you've done it." Edward put on his hat, placed the blood stained razor (the object he had removed from the cupboard) on a chest of drawers before proceeding straight to the police station in Porth, where he was to confess his crime.

At a few minutes to eight in the morning, Edward Davies sat in Porth police station. He was covered in his wife's blood although he may have been oblivious to that fact, as he quite calmly told the duty constable that he had come to give himself up for murdering his wife. "I have cut her throat with a razor. It is all through the Salvation Army. She was bad with Captain Bartly and she was in the family way by him." These were the words that Edward Davies uttered.

After making inquiries and finding that his confession of murder was correct, the police cautioned Edward Davies as to any statement that he might make. To which he replied, " I don't wish to say anything. But I done it, that is the razor. I cut her. There was more blood on it when I left it. but perhaps some came off on my hands by shutting it."

The ensuing court case was short and there was little need for further evidence or witness statements. The coroner in summing up the 'dreadful case' said, "It was not often, he was glad to say, that such shocking occurrences took place among the Welsh hills. The evidence was very plain and he did not think it necessary to comment upon it. There could be no doubt that the wretched man inflicted these wounds on his wife with the razor produced and if they believed the evidence, they (the jury) must bring in a verdict of 'wilful murder'. All he could hope was that certain rumours referred to in the local newspapers as to the prisoner's mind being deranged were true."

The jury did not take long to reach their verdict of "Wilful murder" and Edward Davies was transferred by train to Cardiff Gaol.

The funeral of the late Mrs Davies, as was expected, was attended by thousands of people. She was buried at Llantrisant churchyard in a family grave in which a child of hers had been buried thirteen years before. Strangely enough, it was stated that the grandparents of the murdered were also buried there.

It was also tragically revealed by Dr Ivor Lewis of Cymmer who performed the post mortem on the unfortunate murder victim, that at the time of death, contrary to Edward Davies's belief, his wife was not pregnant.

It is unknown by the authors, as to whether Edward Davies was executed or sentenced to a long term in prison.

MANSLAUGHTER IN PENYGRAIG 1900

Symbolically, Christmas is a time of family gatherings, merriment, rich food and expensive gifts. Especially today in our materialistically orientated society that affords us many 'taken for granted' comforts and luxuries.

Compared to our modern way of living in warm centrally heated houses full of carpets and soft furnishings, life in 1900 was completely different. This was especially apparent in the Rhondda valleys, where the coal industry was in full swing. New pits were springing up everywhere, local population was increasing at a rapid rate as a result of people migrating to the area in order to seek employment in the mines.

At that time poverty was rife, the air was filled with smoke from thousands of coal fires and coal dust coated everything, adding to the dismal dirty grey living conditions that depressed so many whose lives were a constant day to day struggle to survive. Homes were sparsely furnished, floors were of flagstone, and during the night the cockroaches could be heard emerging from the cracks in the floor to scratch around for crumbs of food. With no welfare system in place the difference between working in the savagely hard conditions of the mines and not working at all was the difference between just surviving and starvation.

Christmas for a child was to receive a piece of fruit or a home made wooden toy if they were lucky. Life was hard and the close knit communities worked hard and lived hard lives, causing many to turn to drink.

Henry Morgan and his wife Mary, a Welsh speaking couple who lived in Penygraig and were presumed to have migrated from North Wales for the work in the mines, decided to celebrate the Christmas of 1900 with a pub crawl. Henry, a pedlar, aged 73 and Mary, aged 69 on the 25th of December were seen at various pubs in the locality. This included the

Adare Hotel and the Butchers Arms Hotel in Penygraig, where it seems that the landlord there refused to serve the couple. After spending the day drinking, the couple went home during the late afternoon, at which time Henry Morgan feeling distinctively worse for wear went to bed.

Sometime later in the evening Henry woke up. At 10.30 p.m., a Mr. Dyke visited the house.

While he was there Mary Morgan was kneeling against a bench and Mr. Dyke witnessed her husband Henry stand over her and scream, (in Welsh) "get up or I'll help you to get up." Mr. Dyke not wanting to be caught up in a row that appeared to be starting between the couple left the house.

A short while later a neighbour named Rees was outside in the garden when he heard Henry Morgan shouting at his wife Mary, "Cwm y jawl." "Rise you devil, rise." Rees then heard noises and heard Henry threatening to kill his wife if she did not comply with his wishes and get up. Rees the neighbour then heard banging, which he thought sounded like blows were being struck.

It was, it seems, not uncommon for rows to boil up between the couple, as both were regular drinkers and Henry Morgan was known to be very volatile with his temper when he was in a drunken state. Therefore Morgan Rees was not unduly concerned as to the goings on, he was he later stated in court just curious as to what the row was over this time. After hearing what he thought were blows being struck, Morgan Rees heard Henry go up and down the stairs a few times before leaving the house.

A short time later, Henry Morgan returned to the house. On his return he was in the company of Mr Dyke, who had called earlier that evening. Dyke was quite shocked to find Mary Morgan lying dead on the floor. Immediately Dyke called Morgan Rees the neighbour into the house.

Morgan Rees noted that Mary was lying on the floor with her feet pointing towards the fireplace. She was attired in a chemise and stockings. The neighbour examined her and agreed with Dyke that Mary Morgan was indeed dead.

Henry Morgan at this time told the men that he had been in bed until 11.30 p.m. and that he had got up to find his wife dead. The two men refuted the statement that Henry made, telling him that they had indeed heard him cursing Mary and threatening to kill her if she did not comply with his wishes.

The surgeon, Dr. Thomas Richard Llewelyn of Penygraig, was called and early on the Christmas morning of 1900 he had the unpleasant task of having to examine Mary Morgan's lifeless body.

Dr Llewelyn found external bruising over the right and left eyes. On the left cheek he found two crescent shaped scratches, a large bruise on the right arm extending from the elbow to the wrist. On the centre of the outer arm the skin was torn in two places. The left arm was bruised as were the backs of both hands. The left thigh was badly bruised and the fourth and fifth ribs on the right side of the body were fractured.

Later that same Christmas day Dr Llewelyn performed a full post-mortem on the body. At this examination he found extravasations of the blood, which corresponded with the external bruising. He found a clot of blood on the brain near the left temple. Where the fourth and fifth ribs were fractured the doctor found the lung to be damaged.

The blows heard by various witnesses were consistent with the injuries found by Dr. Llewelyn, who concluded that Mary Morgan had been beaten to death with a blunt instrument.

Police Constable Grubberman arrested Henry Morgan, whereupon he was taken to Tonypandy Police station and promptly charged with the murder of his wife, Mary Morgan. The charge being that he killed her " by beating her about the head and body with a stick or a crutch."

Morgan gave a statement covering his version of events, which included denying that he had killed his wife. A stick found on the fender of the fireplace was presumed by all to have been the murder weapon.

On the 28th March 1901. Henry Morgan was put on trial at the Glamorgan Assizes in Cardiff. Before Mr Justice Bruce Henry Morgan denied killing his wife Mary. Witnesses were called to testify to the characters of the accused and the deceased. It was said that Henry Morgan was as a rule a gentle sort of man, who was quite kind in his nature. However, he had worked as a collier and had been in no less than three explosions. The last explosion he had been in was in 1869.

It was in this explosion that Henry Morgan had lost his leg and had become a cripple, relying on crutches to get about. These facts were taken into account and the charge of murder against Henry Morgan was reduced to the lesser charge of manslaughter. It was on this charge that the jury found him guilty of killing his wife. The judge announced that the crime was committed under terrible circumstances. He also took into account the prisoners age and disabilities when passing sentence. Henry Morgan was sentenced to five years penal servitude for his crime.

A DOUBLE TRAGEDY IN HOPKINSTOWN 1902

On Thursday 3rd April 1902 the Hollybush Inn, situated in Hopkinstown, was quiet with only a few customers enjoying a leisurely drink. Business being slow was expected, as it was the middle of the afternoon. It was due to this lack of custom that the landlord, Horatio Rowlands, could not help but notice the man and woman who entered his premises. He watched as the couple first went into the sitting room and after only being in there briefly, they went on into the tap room, which apart from the couple was empty.

The couple were only in the tap room for about five minutes when two loud shots sounded throughout the Inn. The landlord saw smoke coming from the tap room and decided that he should investigate the matter. As he headed for the door of the tap room two more shots rang out.

The door of the tap room was partially open and when Horatio Rowlands peered inside the room he was shocked to see the woman, Jane Ann Sadler aged 30, slumped dead on the settee.

The man Philip Evans was sitting next to her, he was conscious, but injured. A revolver lay on the floor next to his feet.

The landlord, shocked by the sight that lay before his eyes, immediately shut the door and bolted it. He then retreated to get a doctor and the police, as he did so another shot rang out from inside the tap room.

It was in this small village that paves the way into Pontypridd from the Rhondda valley, that a fatal case of *menange a trois* was enacted out.

Jane Ann Sadler had been married for the last sixteen years. Jane had left her husband just a few weeks before her untimely death in the Hollybush Inn, leaving him in their marital home at 30 Church Street, Porth. Philip Evans, the man who was with Jane Ann Sadler, was an ex - policeman who resided in Pontypridd. A relationship between the couple had started about the time that Jane had left her husband. In the week before her death Jane had it seems broken up her relationship with Philip Evans and had gone back to her husband, with the promise that it was he that she would stay with. During this time an extremely smitten Philip Evans had endeavoured in vain to try and get Jane Ann Sadler to go back with him. It is here that we can only speculate and presume that it may have been through Philip Evans's efforts to pressure Jane Ann that she agreed to meet with him at the Hollybush Inn on that fateful day. No argument was heard between the couple during their brief time in the tap room, perhaps Evans had used the pretence of wanting to talk to Jane Ann to lure her to the inn, we shall never know. Philip Evans it seems could not cope with rejection by his lover so decided that if he could not have her then no-one else would. Indications were that Philip Evans had to a certain extent premeditated the murder of Jane Ann Sadler and his own intended suicide.

A doctor arrived at the Hollybush Inn along with a P.C. Bodger. Jane Ann Sadler was found by the two men to be dead. Death, the Doctor concluded , had in her case been instantaneous due to two bullets that had entered her brain after being fired from a close range.

Philip Evans was alive and indeed able to get off the settee and lie on the floor unaided. Evans himself had two bullet holes in the temple and one in his forehead, his injuries were deemed to be of a serious nature. Before being moved to Porth Cottage Hospital Philip Evans gave a statement to P.C Bodger confessing to the crime of killing Jane Ann Sadler, he also expressed that he wished himself to be dead.

An inquest held at Porth Court in regards to Mrs Sadler's death concluded based on the evidence and Evans confession, that he had killed Mrs. Sadler. Upon his recovery, Philip Evans should be charged with the wilful murder of the deceased. Philip Evans however, was not going to be able to answer to the law for his crime, as just a few days later, he himself succumbed to his self inflicted injuries at Porth Cottage Hospital.

On or about the 8th of April 1902 an inquest was opened into the death of Philip Evans. Dr Roberts who had carried out the post-mortem on Philip Evans, concluded that death was due to pressure on the brain as a result of the presence of three bullets. The coroner, Mr R.J. Rhys questioned witnesses about the tragic affair. Also present to give statements were the brothers of the deceased man. One of the brothers, Frank Evans, stated that after leaving the police force, Philip Evans had left the Glamorganshire area and gone to Ireland. Later Frank had brought his brother Philip home to Waterford. At the time, Philip was found to have a bottle of poison about his person. Frank testified that his brother on times could be very childish and that he had some very peculiar traits to his personality. It was also stated by Frank that his brother Philip had been extremely fond of the woman he had killed.

The jury once all statements had been read, returned with a verdict that found Philip Evans had died from gunshot wounds by his own hand and that he was insane when he committed the act of suicide.

Immediately after the inquest Evans was interred at Lledryn. The funeral was quiet and held in secret. Eight constables did however act as pallbearers and the mourners consisted of Evans's two brothers. With a simple prayer as a substitute for the usual Church of England service, the remains of Philip Evans were laid to rest as part of a tragic love triangle.

THE WOODFIELD HOTEL MURDER 1902

In Wales, criminal behaviour was more often than not blamed on outsiders and foreigners and this attitude could be seen not only among the working classes but also in the middle classes.

Coroners in their statements openly displayed xenophobic views. The Welsh, although not entirely blameless, especially with regard to drink related crimes, certainly had the reputation for being "strangers to the knife and the gun."

Two murder cases that illustrated this strangely happened within two years of each other and also very near to each other. One was the murder at the Bridgend Hotel Pentre in 1904, and the other was at the Woodfield Hotel Pentre in 1902. The Woodfield Hotel was about 300 to 400 yds up the road from the Bridgend Hotel. Both murders involved foreigners and both murder weapons were knives.

The Woodfield Hotel and the Bridgend Hotel have both long since been demolished, but their notoriety through the murders has stood the test of time. Pentre sadly is an area that is becoming well renowned for the number of violent crimes that have occurred in more recent years. These crimes though are more to do with drug abuse, a modern phenomenon.

The Woodfield Hotel which was situated on the right hand side of George Street, a little above a theatre that once stood in Pentre, was busy serving its usual regulars on an afternoon one Monday in April of 1902. There were a mixed group of nationalities, Italians, Irish, English and Welsh. The majority of the patrons were mixing as well in their leisure hours as they did in their working hours down the mines. But as is often the case, the drink being served soon became the catalyst for violence.

The barmaid Edith Griffiths who was a sister of the landlady was in charge of the bar that day.

Edith Griffiths was to serve both the victim Thomas Mackey and his assailant Giovanni Ferrina.

Ystrad Road, Pentre c.1910. The Woodfield Hotel is the large building on the immediate right of the photograph where just a few years before a man was killed in a fight at the premises.

Thomas Mackey, whom Edith knew, was an Irishman originally from Kilkenny. He was a well built man aged about thirty, who lived with his wife and six children who ranged from seven years old down to eleven months old. Thomas lived in Ystrad in a basement beneath a shop at 191 Underhouses on Ystrad Road. Thomas Mackey worked as a night repairer at the Pentre colliery and had been living in the Rhondda for twelve years. He was well liked by his friends, who described him as being a quiet unassuming man, but one who liked his drink. Perhaps it was this fondness for drink that would ultimately lead to his untimely death that day.

Thomas had gone to the Woodfield very early on Monday afternoon and when he had not returned home for dinner, his wife Florence went looking for him. Florence found Thomas sitting in the back parlour of the Woodfield Hotel . Thomas Mackey had had more than a few drinks by then and refused to go home saying he did not intend to go to work that night either.

The next time that Florence was to see her husband again, would be when he lay dying on the floor of the Woodfield Hotel.

The assailant in the affair was an Italian named Giovanni Ferrina, as previously stated.

Giovanni Ferrina until the week before the fatal incident had been working as a labourer at Pentre Colliery, and had resided in lodgings with three other Italians at 22 Tyisha Road Gelli. He had been living in the area for about five years and had a brother Michealo, who was an ice - cream vendor in Cardiff. Ferrina was married with a son aged about sixteen who, together with his mother, were living back in his native home of Italy. Like Mackey, he was considered by friends and family to be quiet, inoffensive and kind hearted, however his one downfall was his quick and fiery temper.

Ferrina had gone drinking in the Woodfield Hotel at about 4 p.m. with another Italian, Joseph Gamara, and a few Englishmen. It was about 6.30 p.m. , not long after Mackey had entered the bar from the back parlour that the fatal affray occurred. From witness statements there seemed to be three main stories which were all conflicting about how the argument between the two men started. One was that a dispute arose over a 'tot' of beer. Another version concerned a quarrel over a game of rings and the third story was that the two men had a heated discussion about the Boer War. It was from witness statements fair to say that the first version was the likeliest cause. Although different people saw things in different ways and the degree of violence that each person is said to have meted out to the other varies according to where the sympathies of the individual witness lay.

In the end it seemed that the argument was over beer. Mackey had pushed or struck Ferrina who had beer upset over him and retaliated by attacking Mackey. A full blown fight ensued between the two men and during the fight Ferrina drew a knife from his pocket and stabbed Mackey. The knife penetrated Thomas Mackey's left thigh, severing the main artery causing a fatal wound from which Mackey succumbed twenty minutes after he had been stabbed.

By the time the police arrived to arrest Ferrina a large crowd had gathered outside the Woodfield Hotel. Sergeants Richards and Morris took Ferrina into custody at Pentre Police station, although by that time Ferrina had been subjected to ' severe handling' from the angry spectators who had seen the events between the two men unfold. Ferrina's face bore a number of disfiguring marks and swellings as a result of his treatment, his face being practically pounded to a jelly.

When Dr. Thomas and Inspector Williams arrived, a scene of carnage awaited them. Mackey lay on the floor bleeding profusely from his thigh. A handkerchief had been bound tightly around the wound. A large quantity of blood covered the floor over an area of four feet by two and a half feet. There were also splashes of blood over the counter and the window.

There was a sense of shock and quiet disbelief among the onlookers who had certainly never anticipated that what had started out as a disagreement over a drop of beer could have resulted in a murder inquiry.

On Wednesday morning the inquest was held at Pentre police station, the district coroner being Mr R.J. Rhys. The interest in the case had meant that a large crowd had gathered outside the police station to hear the verdict. When Ferrina was brought in his face still bore the traces of the terrible beating that he had endured by the crowd of spectators on the day of the murder.

At the inquest, although he did not deny the charge, Ferrina in his defence stated that he had acted purely in self defence when he had found himself surrounded by between twenty to twenty four men. Some of them he claimed were grabbing at his arms and he felt himself in fear for his own life.

After hearing all the witness statements the coroner in summing up thought that the jury had two questions to consider. Those being whether it was a case of wilful murder in that Ferrina intended killing Mackey or was it a case of manslaughter, in that the prisoner acted in self defence? Mr R.J Rhys coroner said that if it was self defence then it did not justify pulling a knife and stabbing someone fatally and in his opinion he "was glad to say, such conduct was rare in this country. Ferrina was a native of a country where one thought very little of drawing a knife for the purpose of self defence...... had he been an Englishman he would probably have fought Mackey in the ordinary way.—- Mackey was the aggressor, but Ferrina is evidently a very excitable man with hot Southern blood in him and he had drunk a little beer as well on the Monday in question."

It took only twenty minutes for the jury to reach a verdict of manslaughter against Ferrina. The immense crowd that had gathered outside awaited the verdict in the hope of seeing the prisoner conveyed to Cardiff gaol.

Thomas Mackey was buried on the following Saturday at Llethrddu cemetery. It seems that because the financial situation of the family was not 'overbright', a public collection was made to defray the expenses of the funeral.

Sadly, Thomas Mackey's brother who had travelled down from Ireland for the funeral had a terrible shock. He had been led to believe that his brother had been killed in a colliery accident.

A FATAL AFFAIR IN PENTRE 1902

This sad and tragic story even though almost a hundred years old, still stirs feelings in those whose families and friends lives were affected by the unfolding of the events on the cold winter,s night of Saturday December 27th 1902, which led to the death of Ethel Adlam on the following day.

Ethel Adlam, a pleasant, seventeen year old young woman, was by all accounts a high spirited girl who was diligent, hard working and a person who was habitual in her nature. Ethel who lived with her widowed mother at 1 Volunteer Street in Pentre, had been for the last four years courting twenty-one year old Tom Lewis, who was employed as a night haulier at the Ocean Colliery Company's Dare Pit in Cwmparc and who lived at 15 Volunteer Street. All indications were that Tom and Ethel were a couple who were very fond of each other, however in later witness statements their relationship was noted to be of a volatile nature in which Tom Lewis on occasion when in temper, it was claimed, had struck out at Ethel, giving her rise to complain to her mother. As a result of this, the relationship on occasions was known to have faltered.

The sequence of events that led to the tragic death of a young girl began on Saturday December 27th 1902.

At about 5.15 p.m. on December 27th, John Barnett arrived at 15 Volunteer Street, the home of his mother, Mrs Jury, who was housekeeper to Tom Lewis and his widowed father. John Barnett may have regretted entering into the house, as he walked into a fierce argument between Tom Lewis and his father. Tom was in a furious temper, so much so that he took a photograph from the wall, tore it up and threw it onto the fire. Tom Lewis later left the house to go drinking in the Griffin Inn. Tom Lewis no doubt spent his time in the public house drowning his sorrows and his temper for a while at least. The Griffin Inn, situated on the main road running through Pentre, was conveniently placed at the junction into

Volunteer street. At 9p.m. Tom had only to walk a few yards from the Griffin Inn to 1 Volunteer Street when he decided to visit his sweetheart Ethel.

Ethel's mother Mrs Adlam answered the knock on the door, upon seeing Tom she invited him into the house. Mrs Adlam noticed that Tom was slightly worse for wear due to his drinking. She found Tom to be in what was later described as, "an excitable state". Tom made references to his dead mother, telling Mrs Adlam that his father had been talking about her. Mrs Adlam had responded to Tom by telling him not to talk about the dead.

Tom Lewis was at the Adlam house for only a few minutes before deciding to leave, via the back door. Ethel followed closely by her mother accompanied Tom to the door. Tom was planning to take Ethel back to the Griffin Inn with him, in order to continue his drinking. However Mrs Adlam, concerned that Tom had drunk enough alcohol, would not allow Tom to go back to the pub. Instead Mrs Adlam escorted Tom and her daughter Ethel to the Lewis household.

At the Lewis household Tom lay on the settee for a time, he then got up, his temper flared and threatened to strike his father. Tom accused his father of killing his mother. Mrs Ellen Adlam with the help of John Barnett somehow managed to keep Tom and his father apart. Once assured that Tom had calmed down, Ethel's mother left the house to return home; the time being about 9.30 p.m.

Shortly after all of these goings on, Tom Lewis left his father's house via the back door. As he left the house Tom called after Ethel to join him. Dutifully Ethel followed Tom. Mrs Jury the housekeeper heard the couple conversing outside for about ten minutes, they then left the yard presumably to go for a walk.

Later evidence showed that Tom and Ethel had after this time been at the ash tip, near where the river ran at the bottom end of Volunteer Street. One can only presume that an argument broke out between Tom and Ethel. From the ash tip, they somehow ended up at the river's edge. It can only be guessed at whether Ethel went to the river's edge voluntarily with Tom or whether she went under duress.

The facts that are known are that at around 11.40 p.m. 15 year old Albert Hoskins of 18 Volunteer Street (the nearest house to the river) retired to his bed. His sleep was disturbed at around midnight, when he heard the frightened screams of a female coming from the direction of the river. Albert Hoskins only disclosed this information after Ethel's body was found, claiming to think little at the time of what he had heard.

The Griffin Hotel where Tom Lewis drank before killing his girlfriend. Volunteer Street is directly behind the Griffin, the houses shown in the background are on the opposite side of the street to where the victim and her killer lived.

Thomas Clark, a signalman at the Tynebedw signal box, also heard the screams of a female at about the same time as Albert Hoskins.

During the time that events were unfolding towards a tragic conclusion at the river's edge Ellen Adlam, who had been expecting her daughter to come home early, became anxious as to where her daughter was. Unable to contain her anxiety Mrs Adlam at around 11 p.m. made her way to the Lewis household. Upon finding that Tom and Ethel were not there, Ellen Adlam began making enquiries at the neighbours' houses. Without any positive news of her daughter's whereabouts, Ellen Adlam made a search of the adjoining streets and adjacent lanes. Her search proving to be fruitless, she returned home.

At around 1 a.m. Sidney Adlam, Ethel's brother, returned home to find his mother in a distressed state due to the fact that Ethel was missing. Sidney immediately decided to search for his sister. A search party was very quickly formed which included Mrs Adlam's other son William who lived in Carne street, William Comley of 8 Volunteer street and Watkin Morris of 18 Volunteer street; Watkin being married to Ethel's sister.

Sidney Adlam's first port of call with the search party was to the Lewis household. Tom and Ethel were nowhere in sight.

At about the same time as the search party was at the Lewis household, William Comley and John Barnett in their search for Ethel found her hat on the riverbank. The two men retrieved the hat and returned to the Lewis household in time to find Sidney Adlam searching around the area of the Lewis household. Sidney repeatedly called out Tom and Ethel's names as he did so.

Around 2 a.m. John Barnett and Sidney Adlam decided to search the backyard of the house. Both were extremely surprised to find Tom Lewis cowering beneath the chicken coop. Tom appeared to be in a dazed state, when Sidney dragged him out from beneath the chicken coop. Sidney demanded to know where his sister was. Tom answered that "Ethel had gone home from him, this long time."

Tom Lewis caught hold of John's hand, apparently in a frightened way. Sidney Adlam headed into the house to arrange for his mother to be sent for. Meanwhile Tom, in a distressed state, told John that "Ethel had gone and done it. She had jumped into the river." Tom claimed that Ethel had lost her temper with him and that she had run away from him and leapt into the river. Tom then urged John to go with him to the river, but then decided that he should tell the others where Ethel was. Tom was led into the house, where by this time Mrs Adlam was waiting for him. In the meantime the police were sent for.

Ellen Adlam immediately began questioning Tom as to her daughter's whereabouts. Tom's reply was, "To tell you straight she is in the river." Mrs Adlam not fully grasping what Tom had just told her pleaded with him to tell the truth about the matter. With that Tom repeated again his statement that Ethel was in the river. At this reply Ellen Adlam fainted and had to be taken home.

It was then decided that Tom Lewis should lead Sidney Adlam and the others present in the room to the river.

At the river's edge Watkin Morris held his pit lamp up in order to see more clearly in the direction that Tom Lewis was now pointing. Before all witnesses present there in the river was the body of Ethel Adlam.

At first it was believed that Ethel was alive, due to the fact that when she was found, her body was in a sitting position, with her head slightly bent to the right. Ethel was placed in water no more than nine inches deep. Her body was clothed, but the clothes had been torn open, causing Ethel to be bare from the waist up. The dark red bodice that she had on, was dirty and bedraggled.

Tom Lewis cried bitterly, begging the still form of Ethel Adlam to speak up and tell those present that he had not done this to her.

Watkin Morris, aided by his brother in law William, carried Ethel's body to the riverbank.

Shortly after 3 a.m. Dr James Clement Reardon arrived at the scene of the crime, followed closely by PCs Alexander and Griffiths and Inspector Williams from Ton- Pentre police station. Dr Reardon estimated that Ethel had been dead for at least an hour, maybe two. On the spot observations made by the doctor noted that the body was lying on its back, slightly inclined to the right . The right arm was level to the shoulder, the left arm was close to the side of the torso. The fingers of both hands were clenched into the palms. The deceased's hair was wet, dishevelled and knotted, with sand, ashes and debris stuck in it. The clothes on the body were in extreme disarray, especially the upper portion, leaving a breast fully exposed.

Inspector Williams arranged for Ethel's body to be removed to the house and arrested Tom Lewis on suspicion of causing the death of Ethel Adlam between 10 p.m. on the 27th December and 2 a.m. on the 28th December. Tom Lewis was then conveyed to Ton-Pentre police station.

At the house Dr. Reardon further examined the remains of Ethel Adlam. He found that over the whole of the right side of the face was extensive bruising, along with two longitudinal cuts of a superficial nature, which were about four and a half inches in length. Grit was embedded in the cuts and the surrounding skin. The left cheekbone was bruised, there were superficial cuts to the forehead, abrasions to the throat and also to the upper part of the chest. On the left side of the mouth was a circular incised wound, which the doctor felt was not a fresh wound. Considerable bruising covered the whole of the right breast, but no broken ribs were detected. The tongue and mouth were coated with sand and the throat was clogged with sand and mud. The eyes were partially closed with one eyelid appearing to be scratched and having the appearance of a black eye. The body also had scratches to the stomach. Upon examination of the lower part of the body, a discharge of blood was noticed.

Tom Lewis once taken to the police station was in front of two police constables formally charged by Inspector Williams with causing the death of Ethel Adlam. Tom Lewis in response to the charge proceeded to make a statement. Tom claimed in his statement that Ethel for some reason unknown to himself had got upset with him. She then according to Tom had started threatening to commit suicide. Ethel, Tom stated ran away from him so he gave chase, concerned by her threats. Tom stated that he caught up with Ethel at the ash tip where nearby building works were underway. Tom claimed that it was at the ash tip that he and Ethel had fallen into a hole. Ethel, he continued, had got up and ran away from him towards the river's edge.

At the river's edge Ethel, Tom further claimed, had fainted. When she fainted, Tom stated, Ethel had fallen doubled up onto her face. Tom claimed that he had picked Ethel up and tried to pull her from the river. In failing to pull her from the water Tom had, he stated, left her in the river in the sitting position that she had been found to be in by the search party. Tom told in his statement that he had been too afraid to tell Ethel's mother what had happened, he decided instead to go and hide underneath the chicken coop.

News of Ethel Adlam's death and Tom's involvement had by now spread around the locality, causing an immense sensation in the district. By all accounts the two families were very well known in the area and indeed were also well respected within the community.

On Monday morning of the 29th December Tom Lewis was brought before the magistrates at the Ton-Pentre police courts. Crowds of people had gathered by now in Volunteer street and at the river, viewing the site where Ethel's body had been found. People also lined the route to Ton-Pentre and milled about outside the Police Courts that adjoined the recently built Police station.

When Tom Lewis was called, the short sturdy red-headed young man took his place on the defendant's stand. Tom paid full attention to the evidence that was offered against him. Before the magistrates, Mr J. Ignatius Williams, Alderman Richard Lewis, Alderman E.H. Davies and Messrs D. W. Davies and J. D. Williams, the witnesses were called to give their evidence as to the events that had occurred on the previous weekend.

In light of evidence given the prisoner Tom Lewis was then formally remanded into custody until Wednesday 31st December. Tom was then removed to Pentre police station in a covered brake. Despite the large crowd that had gathered, no hostile displays were demonstrated towards the accused man.

Just a few hours after Tom Lewis's appearance at the magistrates court, doctors Thomas Reardon, Philips and Brown carried out a post mortem on the remains of Ethel Adlam.

The next morning, Tues. 30th December, at the Queen's Hotel, situated on the main road in Pentre, the coroner held an inquest into the circumstances of Ethel Adlam's death. Mr R.J Rhys (coroner), from Aberdare, presided over the inquest. Included in the attendance list were

Mr Samuel Pugh (foreman of the jury), Mr T. Millar (solicitor defending the accused), Supt. Cole of Pontypridd police station and Inspector Williams of Pentre police station. The accused Tom Lewis was also present but in the custody of P.C. Dagg.

Mrs Ellen Adlam gave her evidence to the coroner, she also identified the clothing that her daughter was wearing at the time of her death. The clothes were quite torn. Ellen Adlam told the coroner that when Ethel had left the house, her clothes were in good condition, except for a small tear on the left side of her corset. Mrs Adlam was shown the corset in question, which had a loose black steel protruding from it. Mrs Adlam on seeing the corset, testified that the corset had not been damaged to the extent that it now was when her daughter had left the house on the night that she died.

After other witness statements Dr Reardon was called to offer his findings of the post-mortem examination. The other doctors who had attended the post mortem were present to hear Dr. Reardon's evidence. The findings of the post-mortem revealed that one of the breasts had darkened and upon opening the victim's windpipe a considerable quantity of frothy fluid was inside. Upon opening the chest, there were found to be congested areas of haemorrhage on the lining encircling the heart. There was a considerable amount of blood in the chest cavity. The right side of the heart was greatly distended and gorged with blood, the left side of the heart was practically empty.

The doctor stated that in his experience these internal damages were indicative of suffocation.

The valves of the heart were normal, the lungs were gorged with blood and very crackled to feel.

Dr. Reardon also established that the victim had just emerged from her menstrual cycle and this accounted for the blood loss in that region of her body. Dr Reardon added that the brain was congested, but there was no fracture to the skull. Again the doctor stated that the findings of the post-mortem were indicative of death being due to suffocation through drowning, adding that the poor girl may have received a blow to the head, causing lapse of consciousness. This was not proved. In respect of the bruised condition of Ethel's face, the doctor thought that it may have been caused by blows to the face during a struggle or caused by a fall. Although without being totally positive, the doctor felt sure that Ethel Adlam had sustained her bruising through blows she had received from the accused, which in his opinion may have caused insensibility on the victim's behalf. The bruising, it was emphasised, was more severe on the right side of the victim's face.

The coroner became concerned and wanted to know whether the grit and dirt found in the victim's throat came from the river or the ash tip. Dr Reardon could not answer the coroner conclusively. All he could say was that it was black stuff in her throat, the substance looking more like that found on an ash tip.

The coroner in summing up stated that the jury needed to ascertain the cause of death. He reminded the jury that Ethel had been found in about seven inches of water. The fact that the victim was found in an upright sitting position with her head clear of the water was relevant.

Consideration also needed to be taken of the fact that her clothes were torn and disarranged, as well as of the amount of severe bruising about the body which indicated that violence had occurred. The fact that Thomas Lewis was quite drunk and argumentative earlier in the evening was also to be noted as he was the last person to see Ethel alive. His (Tom's) earlier state could have been indicative of his state of mood later in the evening. It was indeed also noted how strange it was to find Tom Lewis hiding under the chicken coop, instead of in his house. Although the true events of what occurred between Tom Lewis and Ethel Adlam could only be known by the couple, one of whom was dead, evidence showed that a prolonged struggle had occurred between the couple.

The coroner went on to say that the morning after Ethel's body was recovered, her brooch and hat pin were found at the ash tip, which was en-route to where her hat was found on the river bank. The jury according to the coroner had to act more like a grand jury rather than as a common jury. He then pointed out that it was no business of theirs to acquit Thomas Lewis. The jury had to decide whether Tom Lewis was instrumental in the death of Ethel Adlam or if she had acted alone and committed suicide.

He added that he found it hard to believe that Tom Lewis as he had claimed found it to be impossible to get Adlam to the water's edge, as Ethel Adlam was only 5ft 4 inches tall and not a very largely built woman. Although it was conceded that there had been a heavy rainfall, Ethel had been found in a raised area of the riverbed, which allowed the water to stay shallow at that point.

The jury consulted with each other for about twenty minutes before arriving at their verdict. The foreman then announced the verdict as being one of guilty of murder. The next day Tom was again placed in front of the magistrates, where he was further remanded into custody before being taken to Cardiff gaol to await his trial.

A great deal of sympathy was shown in the locality towards the accused and his father following the arrest. So much so that a circle of friends started a fund in order to alleviate the circumstances of Mr Lewis and to pay towards a decent defence for Tom. William Comley of Volunteer Street sat as treasurer on the committee, and along with others was taking a great interest in the welfare of the unfortunate family. In order to raise money meetings by the committee were held every Wednesday up until the trial, billiard matches were sponsored and even a concert was arranged at the Lyceum Theatre in Pentre.

On Wednesday 7th January 1903 Tom Lewis was brought before the magistrates in Pontypridd.

After hearing more evidence the magistrates confirmed the charges brought against the accused Tom Lewis. Lewis pleaded not guilty to the charges. He was then committed to take his trial at the assizes.

The trial began on the 27th March 1903. Great interest was taken in the trial of Tom Lewis. Tom himself was firmly composed on his entrance into the dock and in a firm voice again pleaded "Not guilty" to the charges against him. Tom showed no signs of emotion as the jury were empanelled. The judge Mr Justice Philimore offered the accused the chance of a seat, the prisoner thanked his Honour accordingly.

Witnesses were called forward to give their evidence accounting all known details of the events of the night in December that led to the death of Ethel Adlam. Again when Dr. Reardon was called he confirmed that death had been due to suffocation by drowning and that a second post-mortem had taken place at the request of the defence. The findings were considered to be the same as the findings of the first post mortem. The cause of Ethel's death was in fact then brought into debate by the judge. Was the drowning accidental or had Ethel passed out and been too weak to raise her head from the water, or had Tom Lewis caused her to drown?

It was suggested to the jury in the summing up by the prosecution that on the night in question Tom in his manner of hiding and subsequent behaviour at the water's edge was of a selfish nature. Nothing in his conduct showed any concern for Ethel's welfare at all. The jury had to consider also the evidence and decide what they considered the circumstance of death to be. It was also pointed out that Tom Lewis was with Ethel at the time of her death. Why then did he not act quickly to save the girl, surely he could have? Once all points were covered in the summing up, the jury retired.

It was at 12.45.p.m. ten minutes later that the jury came back with their verdict. When asked what that verdict was, the reply came back "Guilty of manslaughter, with a strong recommendation for mercy." The judge considered the jury's opinion to be correct.

The judge addressed Tom Lewis who now had begun to weep. The judge told Tom of his agreement with the jury, stating that on the night in question, the drinking he had done must have inflamed his temper, thus causing the loss of one life and the ruination of another. The judge told Lewis that he had no doubts that Ethel Adlam could have been saved with his help. In reference to the jury's recommendation for mercy, the judge was not sure why they felt that he deserved any mercy at all. But due to Tom's age, the judge decided to follow the jury recommendation. Tom Lewis weeped copiously as he was then sentenced to 15 years penal servitude, with the promise by the judge that if he behaved himself in prison, his sentence would be cut to a quarter of its original length.

Showing no sign of collapse, Tom Lewis stood to be led away by the warders. As the judge promised, Tom Lewis was indeed released five years into his sentence.

Postscript.
In conversation with surviving relatives of Ethel Adlam, details of Ethel's death which never apparently emerged publicly in reports were brought to light.

These details if correct, as they are believed to be by the family, highlight even more the tragic nature of the events that occurred on that fateful night in 1902.

In gaining a more personal insight into the circumstances of the events before and after they occurred, one can only have more sympathy and compassion for those involved at the time and for the following generations that still bear a certain amount of painful emotion as a legacy from events enacted many years before.

The family told me that Tom Lewis did apparently love Ethel Adlam very passionately, so much so that he was very jealous of her. On the night of her death, Ethel had been in her job working as a cleaner at the Salvation Army Hall in Pentre. After finishing work, on her way home Ethel stopped outside the Griffin Inn to talk to a policeman that she knew. Tom Lewis it seems saw Ethel talking to the policeman through the window and became very jealous of the attention that Ethel was receiving. This according to the family later caused an argument between the couple. Ethel was not seen alive again.

Another fact not mentioned in any public account or at the inquest was that Tom Lewis smoked a pipe. Neither was it mentioned that when

Ethel's body was found, there were burn marks from the pipe on her body.

It was mentioned at the inquest that Ethel's corset was torn and that a wire was protruding from the corset. What was not mentioned and is commonly believed in the family today, is that while Ethel and Tom were fighting the wire from the corset actually stabbed into Ethel's chest cavity and pierced her heart, thus causing her death. However the verdict of death by suffocation due to drowning was the official verdict and so must therefore stand today as being the correct one.

As for Tom Lewis, whom the Adlam family even today hold a certain amount of protective sympathy for, he did not as stated serve his full sentence. It seems that the great deal of public sympathy surrounding the case contributed to his early release.

Tom Lewis upon his release went to live at Gelli-Galed, where he later married and had children.

However this was not the end of the story, as a few years later a Q.C. published his memoirs in the 'News of the World.' This resulted in Tom Lewis's wife and children finding out about Ethel Adlam's death and Tom's involvement in the affair. This caused a terrible split in the family, culminating in Tom's wife taking the children and leaving him.

Effectively this destroyed Tom's future with his family. Tom did live to a ripe old age, going senile in his later years. Until his own death, Ethel's death came back to haunt him throughout his life. It also caused a great deal of pain and sadness for Tom's family and for Ethel's family.

It is sad that so many victims were created from the events that occurred so long ago, especially as Ethel's family believe that Tom, despite his jealous possessive streak, loved Ethel dearly and did not intend for a moment to shorten Ethel Adlam's life on that fateful night so long ago.

One can only hope that both, who are now laid to rest, are doing so in peace.

THE BRIDGEND HOTEL MURDER PENTRE

It is hard to imagine and believe today, when looking at the site where ninety six years ago a brutal murder caused such a huge sensation and outrage which ultimately caused a man to meet his fate on the gallows, that these events actually happened in our historic past.

The scene which saw its share of tragedy has changed beyond recognition.

Today where once stood the Bridgend Hotel along with other properties and homes that lined the way to Pentre, now stands a public toilet and a lengthy space of land that has grass laid and diamond shaped flower beds that bloom daffodils every spring.

The public toilet marks the spot that separates the two villages either side of it. Pentre, which follows once you pass the naked land that once housed the now demolished buildings of yesterday. Pentre, although a thriving community still today, has lost the commercial side of itself. In the early 1900s shops lined the main road through Pentre. Shops that were busy and thriving with their many customers. As the century wore on, this side of the community was lost as Treorchy a mile or so further up the road became more the centre of the commercial community. Shops eventually lost their trade and became run down. Buildings were demolished or boarded up, leaving part of Pentre looking run down.

On the other side of the public toilets, across the bridge is the village of Ton Pentre, not quite as unlucky as Pentre as far as the commercial side of things is concerned. Ton Pentre today is also a thriving community, with shops and eateries lining the main road through the village that takes you next into Gelli. Although more modern in its appearance, the two villages have not changed a great deal in the last 100 years. Only the people that come and go, like the times and fashions and seasons.

Today the railway station still stands as it did back then, maybe not so busy as it was but it's still there with the track running alongside the river,

The photograph shows the Bridgend Hotel on the immediate right, to the left and out of the photograph is the entrance to the railway station where the killer ran along the track in an effort to escape capture. The bridge, which leads to Ton Pentre, is where crowds arrived to view the site of the murder.

the only difference being that the steam trains of old have long since been replaced with their modern counterparts.

The road that flows through Ton Pentre up over the bridge around Bridgend square up into Pentre has been widened and tarmaced, replacing dirt tracks and cobble stones that once saw horse drawn carts and carriages pulled along them. The old gas street lamps are now electric.

Traffic lights grace the corner where the entrance into the Bridgend Hotel would have been.

Cars and people constantly pass the place where the Bridgend Hotel stood, not realising that every day they pass the spot where a tragedy was enacted, a brutal crime that put a man into the criminal history books as being another murderer who paid his price at Cardiff gaol.

The public toilet and the stretch of bare land beyond give an air of uncluttered openness to the area, a stark contrast to the closely built clutter of buildings that once stood, clouded by the dusty roads and dirty smoky air that left its black residue on everything it landed on, which was at the time a legacy from the many pits in operation. All that has gone now the air is cleaner and the valley brighter. Unlike the valley of many years ago.

But with all that change memories fade and there are not many now who remember the Bridgend Hotel murder or the huge sensation it caused in 1904, which is a small shame, after all no matter how good or bad events in the past are, they still are our history and it is history that shapes our lives whether it be in a small or a big way.

Here follows the story of the Bridgend Hotel murder.

On Saturday September 10th 1904 life for 37 year old Emlyn Jones and his wife Minnie was full of its usual routines. As the licencees of the Bridgend Hotel on Bridgend Square, situated between the small villages of Ton-Pentre and Pentre, they expected to be busy. Even for a Saturday business was very good and as usual the couple were serving customers and busy mingling with the locals, with whom they enjoyed popularity.

The Joneses had previously been the licencees of the Royal Oak Inn, Pontypridd. Emlyn and Minnie, being no strangers to life behind a bar, had obtained the Bridgend Hotel the previous May following the death of Mr F. C. Gould who had been the landlord until his demise. Emlyn Jones a native of Bonvilston, and Minnie his wife of two and a half years, had settled well into the area, enjoying a good reputation of great respectability amongst all who knew them.

The pleasant atmosphere that filled the evening of the 10th September belied the shocking and tragic events that were to unfold during the course of the next few hours.

Unbeknown to Emlyn and Minnie Jones, their movements were being carefully watched by a stranger who in previous days had started to turn up at the bar. In fact on the very evening of September 10th Katie Richards, a niece of the Joneses and also barmaid to them, noticed the stranger again in the bar. The stranger became conspicuous to Katie by his apparent lack of interest in socialising with the other customers present, choosing in fact to stand alone in the corner of the bar to drink his lemonade. Just before 11 p.m. that night the stranger finished his drink and silently left the bar, disappearing through the door and out into the chilly night air.

Once the customers had left the bar the staff spent the next hour clearing up the remains of what had been an enjoyable evening. Once the bar was to Emlyn's satisfaction the staff were allowed to go. Minnie retired to bed at about a quarter to twelve, leaving Emlyn to conclude his business for the evening.

At around 12.15a.m. on the 11th of September, Henry Rees Davies, a butcher, arrived at the Bridgend Hotel with his takings from the shop. (The butcher's shop and the hotel both belonged to the same company. It was Emlyn's responsibility to check that the takings from the shop were in order.) Emlyn Jones counted the takings, noting that the amount totalled £32.00. Henry Rees Davies agreed the amount to be correct and the money was put in the safe at the back of the bar.

After chatting for a while, Henry Rees Davies took his leave and left Emlyn Jones to lock up. Emlyn Jones completed his tasks and now exhausted from his busy evening climbed the stairs to the second floor bedroom where he planned to retire for the night.

The bedroom had two windows, one of which faced out into the back yard. The other window offered a view of the railway line which runs still alongside the river Rhondda.

Minnie Jones was by now asleep, alongside her lay the peacefully sleeping figure of their baby son Clifford. Silently Emlyn undressed, then took his place in bed as carefully as he could in order not to disturb his sleeping family. Exhausted Emlyn took only a few minutes to fall asleep.

On the dressing table a night light burned, casting a soft reassuring glow around the room. The bedroom door stood, as was habit, slightly ajar.

Just after 2 a.m. Mr J.W. Thomas, a grocer living nearby, was woken by the sound of his dog's frantic barking. Upon investigating the cause of the barking, Mr Thomas's attention was drawn to the dark shadowy figure of a man who was walking along the gully which ran between his premises and a hay store nearby. By the time Mr Thomas managed to get to the place where he had seen the man, he found that the man had moved on.

The very next morning Mr Thomas found that his stable yard door had been opened during the night.

It was around 3 a.m. that the shadowy figure seen by Mr Thomas earlier scaled the high gates that led into the backyard of the Bridgend Hotel. Once in the yard the intruder found a ladder lying against a wall. As quietly as possible he propped the ladder against the wall under the toilet window. Climbing the ladder, the intruder soon managed to gain access to the building through the window.

Once inside the building, the intruder stealthily made his way to the bar. There he proceeded to jemmy open the tills, only to find them all empty. The intruder then tried without success to open the safe.

Disappointed by his failure to obtain any money, the intruder made his way to the bottom of the stairs, where after carefully removing his boots and placing them neatly on the bottom step, he proceeded to climb the stairs.

It was about 3.15 a.m. that Minnie Jones, disturbed by a noise, woke from her sleep. Lifting her head from the pillow, Minnie was terrified to see a man in a crouching position at the foot of the bed. The man suddenly aware that Minnie had seen him, lunged at her just as she began screaming and shaking her husband in order to wake him. Minnie was quickly silenced as the intruder meted out a heavy blow to the side of her head with the jemmy bar. Blood poured down the side of Minnie's face as she fell back against the soft pillow. As she fell, blood from Minnie's head injury splattered across the face and clothes of the still sleeping baby Clifford.

In an instant Emlyn was awake and leapt out of bed, whereupon a desperate struggle ensued between Emlyn and the intruder. Despite her head injuries, a badly concussed Minnie courageously tried to help her husband by grabbing the intruder around the throat. During the violently frantic struggle that was taking place, the thick set powerfully built man produced a knife from his hip pocket. Minnie screamed for help as the man thrust the knife into Emlyn, the blow piercing his heart. Within seconds a mortally wounded Emlyn collapsed to the floor.

Minnie desperately tried to hold on to the man, but his strength soon overcame her desperate efforts. He broke free and made good his escape. Still the baby slept, unaware of the terrible events that surrounded him.

During the time of the struggle Katie Richards, Emlyn's niece who was living on the premises in one of the rooms above, woke to the sound of Minnie's screams. Quickly Katie leapt out of her warm bed and threw open the bedroom window. Desperately she called through the window for help. Seeing no-one outside Katie rushed to the Jones's bedroom, where she was told of the attack. Katie ran back to her room, put her head through the window and again for all she was worth screamed for help.

The head barmaid, Miss Morgan, who shared the room with Katie Richards, was herself now fully awake. Miss Morgan was unsure as to whether it was the terrible screaming that woke her or the sound of the intruder as he fell with a bang down the steep stairway during his desperate efforts to escape.

Jack 'the boots' Carpenter, also a resident and the cellarman at the hotel, was himself now fully awake and was scrambling about putting his trousers on in order to investigate the cause of all the commotion.

When Jack 'the boots' finally reached the Jones's bedroom, he found Minnie on the landing near to the bedroom door. Emlyn Jones was slumped in the corner on the floor, moaning and apparently unconscious. Minnie in her state of panic managed to tell Jack that she and her husband had been attacked and that she thought Emlyn to be seriously hurt. Jack 'the boots' rushed to the slumped form of Emlyn Jones in order to support him.

At the same time that Jack 'the boots' was aiding Minnie and Emlyn, Katie Richards saw two wagons being drawn along the road. Frantically she called to catch the driver's attention, pleading with them to fetch the police and call a doctor. One of the men shouted back at Katie, telling her that if she fetched a doctor they would fetch the police.

Katie ran down the stairs to find Jack 'the boots' supporting Emlyn Jones. Jack told Minnie to take his place at her husband's side, while he accompanied Katie to bring a doctor. Minnie Jones complied, holding her husband in her arms. Just moments later in a barely audible whisper, he uttered the words, "Oh Minnie, Oh baby." The screams of his son, who had now awakened, echoed around the room.

Miss Morgan the head barmaid viewed the scene from the bedroom door. Horror and disbelief filled her at the sight of Minnie, her face caked in blood, cradling Emlyn in her arms; the baby screaming as he lay covered in his mother's blood. Minnie Jones screamed at Miss Morgan to fetch some brandy. Miss Morgan obediently complied.

From the time of the initial attack on the Joneses until the time that Miss Morgan went to fetch the brandy for Minnie, fifteen minutes had passed.

First on the scene of the tragedy was P.C. Rowe who, as carefully as possible, managed to get Emlyn Jones onto the bed. Shortly after, Jack 'the boots' arrived and asked P.C. Rowe to check the building as he could see no sign of the intruder. Jack 'the boots' stayed with Minnie and Emlyn. A few minutes later Emlyn Jones succumbed to his injuries. Poor Minnie, for the second time she became a widow (her first husband had been Mr Maybery Thomas).

Shortly after P.C. Rowe arrived at the scene of the crime, Inspector Williams and other police officers from Ton-Pentre police station arrived. An investigation was immediately effected by the officers. Upon inspection of the premises, a pair of brown boots were found at the bottom of the stairs along with a cap, and a jemmy was found in the bedroom. It was found that the intruder had entered the premises through an

Reconstruction of the Court House. Actual Dock Lnag would have stood in when standing trial. (courtesy of R.A.I.D. Museum).

unlatched toilet window before proceeding through the passageway to the bar. The police quickly ascertained that the intruder who was now a killer had left the building following the same route he had used to enter it.

Despite the fact that Minnie Jones was too distressed to give a description of the attacker, the police with great promptness and efficiency made use of a new private telephone to alert within minutes other police stations based within a twelve mile radius of the crime scene to be on the lookout for the killer. (The telephone system had been inaugurated by the chief constable, making it possible without going through the exchange, to make contact with Pontypridd and sixteen other police stations in the area.)

It was a few short hours later that P.C David Williams (472) and P.C. Woods (235), officers from Pontypridd who were stationed at the old tramway near to the Merlin Hotel, caught sight of a man coming swiftly around the bend of the railway line opposite the Merlin Hotel. The officers' suspicions aroused, P.C. Woods being in plain clothes hid by a signal box above an embankment, while P.C. Williams maintained a position beneath the embankment. When the man arrived at the signal box P.C. Woods pounced on him, much to the man's surprise. P.C. Woods informed the man that he was a police officer, upon hearing this the man put his hand behind his back. P.C. Woods gave a signal to P.C. Williams and grabbed the man. P.C. Williams rushed to the aid of his colleague. The man was secured and taken to Pontypridd police station.

The police officers at the station noted that the man seemed to be in a highly charged state.

Upon examination of the man the police found him to have bloodstains on his face, the back of his head and on his coat. He was without boots and a hat and he had a very nasty wound on his knee. The police at Pontypridd immediately became suspicious that the man they had in custody might be the attacker being sought by them in connection with the murder a few hours earlier. The officers searched him, finding in his possession a clam knife and a putty knife, (with a sharp point and blunt edge). Following the search of the man and the finding of the knives the police charged him on suspicion of having murdered Emlyn Jones.

The prisoner proceeded to give his name and age as being Eric Lange, aged 30 years. He stated that he was a Norwegian sailor belonging to a ship called 'Patricia' which he said was lying in the West Dock at Cardiff. The police in Cardiff were notified of the events that had occurred. Upon making enquiries they found that no such ship was lying in the West Dock. Only a small steamer called the 'Patria' had been docked there and it had set sail on Saturday night.

Eric Lange, who was thickly set, overly built for his medium height, with light hair, a ruddy complexion and blonde moustache, proved to be obstinate. It was with difficulty that the police managed to get him to enter the cab that was to transport him back to Ystrad station.

At Ystrad station, it took two policemen great effort to carry Eric Lange the 300 yards back to Ton Pentre police station, where he was duly confined in the cells.

Later on the same morning of the murder, Sunday 11th September, Mrs Minnie Jones accompanied by her brother and Miss Katie Richards arrived at Ton-Pentre police station.

Despite the terrible grief suffered by the exhausted Minnie Jones she identified Eric Lange from a line up of six men.

By now news of the terrible crime that had been committed at the Bridgend Hotel had spread throughout the Rhondda Valley. Thousands of people flocked from all parts of the valley to congregate on the bridge that divided Ton Pentre from Pentre and outside the Bridgend Hotel itself, in an effort to view the scene of such a terrible crime. From the bridge the ladder which the killer Eric Lange had placed against the window, could be seen. Monday 12th September was by all accounts a dark day, beset by a downpour of rain which added to the gloomy atmosphere that had been cast by the previous day's events. Despite the bad weather hundreds of people gathered outside the Ton Pentre magistrates court filling the surrounding streets, Maindy Road and Maindy Crescent, with their presence as Eric Lange was brought before the magistrates. Those unable to gain admission to the overfilled court waited outside, hoping to catch a glimpse of the accused man.

At about 11.30 a.m. Superintendent Cole called Eric Lange. Before the presiding magistrates Mr T.P Jenkins (chairman), Alderman W. Morgan, Alderman E.H. Davies, Alderman Richard Lewis, Mr J.D. Williams and Mr David Thomas, Eric Lange stood to face the bench. His skin was pale and due to his knee injury he had to cling to the rail of the dock for support. Despite this his lips were pressed tightly shut and determination filled his face.

During the day's proceedings Mr Charles Matthews (solicitor to Pontypridd and Rhondda Licenced Victuallers' Association) supporting the prosecution on behalf of the widow called one by one all witnesses relevant to give evidence. The witnesses included Katie Richards, Miss Morgan, Jack 'the boots' Carpenter, Mr Thomas the grocer, and police officers attached to the investigation.

Once all the evidence was heard the magistrates' clerk turned to the accused Eric Lange and asked him if he had anything to say. In a low voice Eric Lange replied "No". Superintendent Cole then asked for a week's adjournment, stating that the inquest had been fixed for Tuesday 13th September at 1p.m. The chairman allowed the adjournment and remanded Eric Lange for a period of one week.

On the evening of the Monday Dr W. E. Thomas (Ystrad), assisted by doctors Philips (Ystrad) Naunton Morgan (Gilfach) and Joyce (Porth) gathered together and carried out a post mortem examination on the deceased, Emlyn Jones.

At Ton Pentre police station on the 13th of September the inquest into the death of Emlyn Jones was formally opened before Mr R.J. Rhys, coroner. A jury had been empanelled and the proceedings were overseen by Superintendent Cole on behalf of the police. Again the court was filled with spectators and the police had to control the hundreds of people who thronged the streets outside.

The prisoner sat in the dock, apparently calm, collected and in full control of himself.

Minnie Jones, the widow, sat to the right of the coroner. Minnie was dressed in deep mourning, with a veil covering her face. Despite the veil a plaster could clearly be seen on her temple, showing where the prisoner had struck her a blow.

Minnie Jones was called to give evidence as to the events leading up to her husband's death.

With great dignity she did so. Following Minnie's evidence, other witnesses to the events were called to state their roles in the tragic event that had occurred.

Dr W.E. Thomas was then called. His testimony showed that upon arrival at the Bridgend Hotel he found Emlyn Jones to be unfortunately dead. The doctor stated that he had made a superficial examination of the body and had found an incised wound over the region of the heart.

Referring to the post-mortem examination, Dr. Thomas stated that the body of Emlyn Jones had a superficial wound of three quarters of an inch in length on his right forearm. Above this wound was a small puncture wound and slight bruising, which Dr Thomas believed was caused by a bite. On the left arm was a wound and several scratches. The fourth finger of the left hand had a deep lacerated wound which extended to the bone. The fatal wound was a clean-cut wound, of about an inch in length, over the area of the heart. The weapon, Dr. Thomas stated, had pierced through the cartilage to the seventh rib at the junction to the breast bone and had then pierced the victim's heart. The doctor stated that he believed that the fatal wound had been delivered by the putty knife found in Eric Lange's possession rather than the clasp knife which had also been found on the prisoner.

Police Inspector Williams gave his evidence, stating that the boots he had found at the scene of the crime were of a size seven and when they were tried on the prisoner Eric Lange it was found that they fitted him perfectly. The cap found in the bedroom also fitted the prisoner. The prisoner, Inspector Williams related, did not deny that the hat and the boots were his own. The inspector also stated that when the prisoner was charged with burglary Eric Lange replied, "I went in for the money, but could not find any in the bar." When then charged with the murder of Emlyn Jones the prisoner confessed his role in the events of the 11th September. Eric Lange indicated that he also had an accomplice to the crime. However the presence of an accomplice was later dismissed as a lie of Eric Lange's by the presiding coroner.

In summing up the evidence the coroner commented upon how terrible the struggle must have been on that fateful night. He also commended the police in their efficiency at making such a quick arrest. It took just ten minutes for the jury to return with their verdict of wilful murder, the jury being unanimous in their decision. The coroner agreed with the jury's findings.

After conveying deepest sympathy to the widow, the coroner stated, "It was most gratifying to the public of the Rhondda to know that in this as in former instances, the murder had been committed, not by one of themselves, but by a foreigner." (Eric Lange being of Russian descent and not of Norwegian descent as he had stated.)

It was then decided to keep the prisoner overnight in the adjoining police cells, whereupon the next morning he was to be transported to Cardiff prison.

On Thursday 15th of September during the late afternoon the funeral of Emlyn Jones took place at Glyntaff cemetery in Pontypridd. A mass of people lined the route between the Bridgend Hotel and the station. Again at the cemetery a large amount of mourners were present. The service itself was conducted by no less than five ministers, spoken in Welsh, the service was kept brief. So marked the tragic end of John Emlyn Jones.

On Monday November 28th 1904 Eric Lange stood trial at the Glamorgan assizes, Swansea.

The apparent 'nerves of steely composure' previously shown by Eric Lange at the Ton Pentre magistrates court were now replaced with eyes displaying a look of sheer terror and a quivering jaw. On this occasion Mrs Lange was present at the court, accompanied by her young son who, in innocence of the proceedings around him, contentedly ate sweets.

It was only later that Minnie Jones realised that she had travelled on the same train as Mrs Lange (the 7.15 a.m. from Cardiff). The two women had passed each other on Landore station. At that time, neither realised who the other was.

When asked how he pleaded to the charges against him, Eric Lange pleaded 'not guilty.' As witnesses were called to give their evidence the prisoner became more upset, having finally to be held by two warders. On occasions Eric Lange would jump from his seat sobbing and shaking. Once all the evidence had been given by witnesses to the events of September 11th the case for the Crown was closed.

One more witness was called to the stand. Mrs Annie Lorenz Lange. She testified that Eric Lange, her husband, was the father of her three children and that they lived in Middlesborough.

Mrs Lange stated that after losing his job her husband Eric became 'strange in the head.'

After Mrs Lange's testimony was heard Dr Biggs, 'acting medical officer at Cardiff Gaol' stated that in his opinion the prisoner was totally sane and responsible for his actions on the night in question.

The Judge later summed up the evidence. The jury retired at 4.40 p.m., returning at 5.07 p.m.

The verdict was 'Guilty of wilful murder'. Eric Lange met this verdict in a fully composed state.

The judge donned his black cap and passed sentence on the prisoner. "........... I order that you be taken from this place to a lawful prison, thence to a place of execution. That you be hanged by the neck until you are dead and that your body be buried in the precincts of the prison. May God have mercy on your soul."

Lange was then removed from the court and taken to Cardiff gaol to await his punishment.

On December the 8th Eric Lange wrote a letter to Mrs Jones begging for her forgiveness. Needless to say he received no reply. Lange's demeanour apparently changed dramatically. He became depressed and talked about God a lot. After failing to secure a reprieve he resigned himself to his fate.

Lange's wife and three children visited him on the 20th of December. A touching scene ensued when the young children were informed that they would not see their father again on this earth.

Lange wept copiously as he kissed each one of his children for the last time.

The execution of Eric Lange took place on December 21st 1904 three clear Sundays after sentence was passed (waiting three Sundays before carrying out hanging was traditional).

Eric Lange's executioner was one of the Billingtons, (whether it was William, Thomas or John Billington is unclear) who was aided by his assistant John Ellis (who later became an executioner for 16 years from 1907 - 1923).

The press were allowed to watch the execution, which took place in a small shed adjoining 'A' block. It must have been a dismal scene that met the eyes of Eric Lange at a few minutes to eight in the morning, the death chamber lit by a single flickering gas jet attached to one of the whitewashed walls casting an eerie glow around the room. The sight of the hanging rope suspended from a cross beam must have instilled terror into Eric Lange's already fear filled heart. The realisation of the finality of his fate surely must have gripped him as at one minute to eight John Ellis pinioned him, while at that moment one of the warders left the death chamber and held his hand up to the watching press.

Immediately an eerie silence fell about Cardiff prison. Lange was placed into position over the trap, his executioner Billington drew the noose around Lange's neck and placed on his head a white cap. The chaplain said the words "I know that my redeemer liveth" ; at that same moment Billington stepped back, pulled the lever and Eric Lange fell to his death. The sentence had been carried out.

Throughout the lead-up to the trial of Eric Lange, inquiries were made by the police as to his past history. The inquiries revealed that Eric Lange was not the prisoner's real name. Even though his real name was found to be Eugen Lorenz he was still tried by the name of Eric Lange.

The most surprising discovery made, however, was that Lange had at one time actually been employed at the Bridgend Hotel as a billiard marker. This employment had been during 1901, Lange having been employed by the previous landlord Mr. F.G. Gould.

When police searched Lange's home in Middlesborough, documents were found showing that Lange had been born in 1876 and had spent the greater part of his life in Germany. References were also found at the house indicating the satisfaction of Mr Gould with the work that Lange carried out for him in the five weeks he was employed at the Bridgend Hotel.

Those who knew Lange stated, that he was until the time of the murder considered to be of seemingly good character, quite reserved and a gentleman. Lange's wife praised him as a husband and a father, claiming him to be a good provider. Minnie Jones, in her experience of Lange, probably would have strongly disagreed with the statements of good character for Lange. Widowed for the second time she left the Bridgend Hotel on the 30th September 1904, taking her baby son with her. Minnie Jones moved into her mother's house in Pontypridd. Poor Minnie, she must have spent her last weeks in the Bridgend Hotel in utter torment. Living each day there with the memories of the night when her husband was murdered.

Eric Lange's wicked and profitless deed left behind two widows and four orphans, who would for their own lives be his victims, none ever being allowed to forget what Eric Lange had done.

TREHERBERT TRAGEDY 1906

A report which appeared in the Saturday February 17th 1906 issue of the 'Rhondda Leader' had the unusual sub-heading "Done to death with an umbrella." The story concerned a fatal assault upon 43 year old Robert Lloyd, a timberman's labourer who resided at 16 Taff Street Treherbert.

Robert Lloyd had been living in Treherbert for five years and was married to Sarah Lloyd. The couple had five children. Robert Lloyd was a well-respected man, who had been a band sergeant in the South Staffordshire Regiment for 21 years prior to his living in Treherbert. Robert Lloyd enjoyed cricket and music and was a member of Treherbert Orchestral Society.

On the evening of Saturday the 10th February 1906 Robert went to the Railway Hotel in Treherbert for a few drinks with friends. The Hotel was full that evening as it usually was on a Saturday. A lot of the custom was generated from people coming in and out from the local theatre. Two of the regulars who were in the Railway Hotel that night were William Philips aged 30 and his elder brother James aged 36. The two brothers were well known to Robert Lloyd and James it seems was on quite friendly terms with him, the two men often going out together.

However, on this particular night, William Philips got into an argument with a David Evans over beer and William pushed David Evans off the stool he was sitting on. David Evans, was a man of diminutive stature and was indeed known locally as 'Dai Bach'. It was this cowardly act of Williams picking on a smaller man that angered Robert Lloyd. This led to an extremely angry exchange between him and William Philips. A few blows were exchanged, which prompted the landlord of the Railway Hotel, Mr J.M Ryan, to order the two men off the premises immediately. By now William's elder brother James who was sitting at the end of the bar became involved and told William, "Will, get out of this, go home." All three then left the Railway Hotel.

The argument between the two men continued outside on the street . The evidence from witnesses who observed the fight outside was

Site of the Railway Hotel, now demolished.

conflicting due mainly to the speed at which the fatal strike was made. But all the witnesses did agree that although William and Robert were squaring up to a fight, no blows were exchanged outside.

Charles Culverhouse, a friend of Lloyd's, had been standing in front of him trying to persuade him not to continue the fight when suddenly he "heard a whizzing sound passing his ear and saw something strike Lloyd in the eye." Robert Lloyd immediately fell backwards and sank to the ground bleeding profusely from the forehead, nose and mouth. Charles Culverhouse also noticed that Lloyd's "eye was out." Robert Lloyd bled to death on the pavement outside the Railway Hotel without emitting a sound. The shocked bystanders, not realising the seriousness of the injury, tried to lift Lloyd up and get him to answer them, but there was to be no response so they carried his body to his home which was nearby. From Lloyd's house Dr Williams was summoned.

On the following Monday, William Phillips and James Philips were brought to Ton Pentre police court and there were charged jointly with the murder of Robert Lloyd. William Phillips the younger brother was married with one child and living in Wyndham Street, Tynewydd.

James Phillips was single and still lived with his parents at 99 Dumfries Street Treherbert.

The inquest, which took place at Treherbert police station, was conducted by the coroner R. J. Rhys. The solicitor for the defence was a Mr T. Millward, who was one of the most popular and professional men in the Rhondda. Mr Millward had originally started his working career as a collier and had changed his profession with apparent success. As it turned out for the two brothers, their choice of solicitor proved to be most fortunate for them.

It was at the inquest that Dr D.C. Williams was to give his sensational and damming evidence with regards to the post-mortem examination that he had performed on Robert Lloyd.

The Doctor had removed the skull cap and had found the covering of the brain and also the brain itself to be in a healthy condition. Upon removing a triangular bone above the eye, he found a quantity of fluid mixed with blood. There was a fracture on the spheroid bone and he also found that the bone had been fractured all along the wound. The furthest fracture was about three inches from the external wound and in the course of this opening, at a depth of an inch and a half from the external wound, he found an umbrella ferrule and a leather washer. The cause of death was shock and haemorrhage from the wound.

When asked by the coroner whether it would require a considerable amount of force to drive an umbrella into a man's head and leave these items behind he replied "yes.". The umbrella that had caused the fatal wound had been seen in James's possession on that night and had also been recovered from his house later by P.C. David Davies and was brought by him to the inquest as evidence, with the ferrule missing from the end.

In summing up the coroner stressed to the jury that they should only be concerned with events that took place outside the hotel and although the witnesses' stories were rather conflicting, their prime concern should be whether both men were guilty or only one. Murder was out of the question as there was no proof that they were acting from any malice aforethought. After only a few minutes William was aquitted but James was found guilty of 'manslaughter' and remained in custody until the trial.

The sensation the case aroused among the local population was also reflected in the crowds that attended Robert Lloyd's funeral. The streets through which his body was conveyed to Treorchy cemetery were thickly lined with people paying their last respects. 'Thousands having congregated together to watch the closing chapter in the grim tragedy.' Such was the response that several of the local collieries had suspended work at mid-day for the colliers to attend. A subscription fund had also been started to raise aid for the widow and five children and many events were later held to help raise money.

The final chapter to this tragedy took place at the Glamorgan assizes in Cardiff where James Phillips stood in the dock charged with the manslaughter of Robert Lloyd. Mr Lloyd Morgan M.P. (instructed by Mr W. T. Davies of Porth) conducted the prosecution and Mr G. T. Evans K.C., M.P. and Mr Ivor Bowen (instructed by Mr. Millward, Pentre) conducted the defence. James was to plead not guilty. At first, all the evidence seemed to go against James in that the witnesses statements, although conflicting slightly, all agreed on the major point that it was James who had struck the fatal blow with his umbrella. Dr. Williams had even demonstrated, in a dramatic fashion, exactly how the injuries were caused by using a model skull. However, Mr Millward's defence was a powerful one and much sympathy was gained for James Phillips when it was learnt that he had recently returned from working in America, where having to work in water in the mine he had contracted blood poisoning in the leg and had ever since used the umbrella to aid his walking, finding it less embarrassing than a walking stick. Much was made too, of his supposedly long and excellent friendship with the dead man. Thus the jury were led to ask with James's disability, how could he have harmed Lloyd when he did not have the physical ability to do so and would also be disinclined to break a long and established friendship?

Mr Ivor Bowen, for the defence, referred to the 'tragic' circumstances of the case and impressed upon the jury that, "The unfortunate affair was purely an accident", in that Lloyd in a "drunken state" had "staggered and fell so as to come in contact with the umbrella and thus received the injuries which unfortunately caused his death."

It seemed that past evidence from witnesses' statements at the inquest had been largely forgotten, in particular that when cross examined, the landlord of the Railway Hotel, Mr. J.M. Ryan, had stated that Robert Lloyd and the two Phillips brothers were sober. "....if one had had more than the other it was James Phillips." Also Charles Culverhouse, who had been standing next to Lloyd in the street, had said in his statement that "Lloyd fell backwards" when the umbrella had struck him.

The jury after just one minute returned their verdict of 'Not guilty' and James Phillips walked out a free man though not before he had had a warning and a lesson from the judge, who told him "He had unfortunately, under circumstances which were accidental, caused the death of a man who had been his friend. It was to be hoped this would be a warning to him to keep off the drink."

THE TAFF VALE RAILWAY TRAGEDY 1906

On Saturday 20th November 1906 the 9 p.m. train from Treherbert was making its usual run through the winding Rhondda Valley. Travelling on the train to their respective destinations were a 36 year old Miss John of Rheola Terrace Trehafod and a Mr Francis Gear of North Street Porth. Each innocently travelled towards their homes unaware that a tragedy was about to unfold before their eyes, leaving them with a nightmarish memory of their night's travel for many years to come.

To begin the story we must travel back some two months earlier when events that were to culminate in a woman's death began.

At 7 Morgan Terrace in Porth lived Margaret Jones, a woman who was married but separated from her husband John. John Jones lived in Treorchy. Margaret Jones had lived in Morgan Terrace for five years with her presumed lover George Philips, a collier.

It was during this time that a labourer by the name of Scratton became a regular visitor to Morgan Terrace. As a result of Scratton's visits, Margaret Jones struck up an affair with him, which resulted in Margaret Jones leaving forty nine year old George Philips and going to live with Scratton in Newport. These events occurred sometime during the month of August.

Margaret Jones lived with Scratton for about three weeks before she then entered service as a chambermaid at the New Inn in Pontypridd. Margaret's behaviour, it seems, was severely resented by George Philips and this resentment grew ever worse over a period of time.

On the night of October 20th, Margaret Jones and Scratton arranged to meet at Treherbert.

Somehow George Philips found out about the meeting arranged by the couple. As a consequence of this, when the train pulled into Ystrad station, (on its way to Treherbert) at 6.14 p.m., Margaret Jones complained that Philips was "shadowing her". As a result of this complaint, a guard and a policeman intervened and Margaret Jones continued her journey while a disgruntled George Philips returned to his lodgings in Porth.

Scratton and Margaret Jones later boarded the 9 p.m. train from Treherbert. George Philips, still stinging with his resentment, must have been loitering on Porth station, as he saw the couple on the train as it pulled into the station. George Philips got onto the train, entering the carriage being used by Margaret Jones and Scratton along with the two witnesses to the impending disaster, Miss John and Mr Gear.

George Philips immediately proceeded to start a fierce argument with the couple, which very quickly inflated to become a violent struggle between Philips and Scratton. The time was now 9.37 p.m. and the train was in full speed heading for Trehafod station.

Philips punched Scratton to the floor of the carriage and when Margaret Jones protested that he should stop the assault Philips turned on her, viciously punching her about the head and face. In all about ten to twelve times he rained punches on her.

Margaret Jones fell backwards onto the seat, her face was covered in blood. Philips returned to his attack on Scratton.

During this time Mr Gear was desperately trying to shield Miss John from the explosion of violence being committed before them. Francis Gear noticed that, sometime during the struggle that was still in progress, the window of the carriage door had been smashed. He also saw Philips's hands covered in blood.

Whether Margaret Jones was dazed and unaware of her actions due to the blows she had received, or whether she was compelled to act irrationally through sheer terror, can only now be speculated upon. But while the two men continued to fight, Margaret Jones opened the door. Francis Gear shouted at the men, telling them, "She's got out of the door." Philips who was still on top of Scratton on the floor shouted at Scratton to " Bloody well go after her." The fight between the men continued all the way to Trehafod.

At Trehafod station Mr. Gear informed the station-master of the drama that had occurred on the train. P.C. Lucas was called and when informed of the situation he arrested George Philips.

Margaret Jones, upon falling or jumping from the train, was found to have been hit by a mineral train passing alongside. William Brad the mineral train guard was shunting on the down line at Celyn between Porth and Trehafod when he felt a slight jerk. He stopped the train and went back to see what it was that had caused this, it was then found to be Margaret Jones. She was still alive and in a pitiful condition. Both of Margaret Jones's legs and one of her arms were almost completely severed from her body. The barely conscious woman was attended by a doctor from Porth before being transported to Cardiff Royal Infirmary, where a Dr. S.H. West took over her care.

In the meantime George Philips was taken to Porth Police station where he was charged with causing grievous bodily harm to Margaret Jones. However, ten hours after the appalling incident had occurred on the train, Margaret Jones mercifully succumbed to the horrific injuries that she had sustained.

The next day George Philips was taken to Ystrad magistrates court in Ton-Pentre, where the charges against him were altered to 'causing the death of Margaret Jones.' George Philips appeared to be totally unconcerned by this turn of events, while Scratton was totally distressed by his lady friend's death. Scratton related to a pressman that his intention had been to marry the deceased woman at a later date.

At the inquest George Philips had a manslaughter verdict brought against him, resulting in him being committed to the assizes for trial. George Philips was granted bail pending his trial, this being set on provision of £100 and two sureties of £40 each. Bail was only allowed on the grounds that the coroner was sure that Philips had not pushed Margaret Jones physically from the train.

George Philips surrendered his bail to appear on Friday 23rd November at the Glamorgan assizes in front of Mr Justice Watton.

It was stated at the trial that the five year relationship between Philips and Margaret Jones had been an unhappy one to say the very least. This was on the grounds that Philips had been very cruel in his behaviour towards Margaret. It was as a result of this cruelty that the relationship between Margaret and Scratton developed.

After vivid accounts of the circumstances leading up to and then the drama directly before Margaret Jones's death were given by the witnesses present, the judge summed up the evidence.

The judge then directed the jury to consider the evidence before reaching their verdict, which duly came back as "Guilty of Manslaughter."

The judge in passing a sentence of six months' hard labour on George Philips took into account many testimonials submitted on his behalf, one of those being from Mr W. Abraham (Mabon) M.P.. These testimonials indicated that apart from his domestic problems Philips was of an excellent character.

A CRUEL DEATH IN TREHERBERT 1907

On Monday the 15th of July 1907 Mrs Elizabeth Roberts of Ynyswen Road, Treherbert, for some reason had decided to throw a party at her house that evening. A number of Elizabeth Roberts's neighbours were invited.

The party started as expected and a pleasant happy evening was spent by the host and her friends. They drank alcohol and played cards before later taking pleasure in singing and dancing. In fact a good evening was being had by all present.

In attendance at the party was one Thomas Edwards, a single man, who was a native of North Wales. Thomas Edwards, a sinker by occupation, was a lodger who had been residing in the Roberts household for the past twelve months.

Exactly how events unfolded is not quite clear. However it seems that later on in the evening, about the time that the singing and dancing was underway, which was around 10 p.m., Thomas Edwards danced with one of the women who had been invited to the party. For reasons only known to Elizabeth Roberts, she took exception to her lodger dancing with her friend.

Elizabeth Roberts became very annoyed with Thomas Edwards quite suddenly and proceeded to have words with him. Edwards exchanged remarks with his landlady, which caused a venomous argument to erupt between them.

During the course of the argument Elizabeth Roberts in her temper threw a cup at Thomas. As the quarrel broke out John Roberts Elizabeth's husband, was standing at the front door of the house. Hearing the racket inside he turned and went to the source of the row. He entered just in time to see his wife turning to go down the stairs to their basement kitchen. But just as Elizabeth was turning to go down the stairs, Thomas Edwards grabbed a lit oil lamp from the mantlepiece and threw it at Elizabeth.

To the horror of all those present the oil lamp hit the back of Elizabeth's feet and smashed. A wall of flames immediately rose up Elizabeth's skirts, causing her to be almost instantly engulfed in a ball of flame which the oil had ignited. Before the flames could be extinguished Elizabeth Roberts suffered the most terrible agonising burns to her body.

Dr. D.C. Williams was called a short while after the incident and came immediately to attend to the victim's burns. Dr. Williams found Elizabeth Roberts sitting on the side of a bed in a tiny room. Two women were with her. They were tending to Elizabeth by applying flour to some of the burns. Upon examining Elizabeth, the doctor found her to be burnt over an extensive part of her body, she was also in a deep state of shock. The doctor realised immediately that the burns were of a fatal nature to his patient and informed the police accordingly. Major J.S. Davies later read depositions from Elizabeth, which were recorded due to her inevitably impending death.

Elizabeth Roberts suffered a slow torturous death. She languished overnight and throughout the whole of Tuesday, before finally succumbing to her terrible burns on the Tuesday night of the 16th July. In her depositions Elizabeth Roberts, in all decency, afforded some of the blame to herself in respect of starting the argument that led to the following events.Thomas Edwards was immediately arrested following Elizabeth's death and was charged with causing her death.

The inquest into the death of Elizabeth Roberts was held at Treherbert police station on Thursday 18th July.

Evidence was heard relating to events of the night in question and a verdict of wilful murder was returned against the accused Thomas Edwards. Edwards was remanded in custody in order to be brought up and charged on the following Monday at Ystrad magistrates court.

The proceedings at Ystrad magistrates court took place as scheduled. Witnesses were called and the victim's depositions were read out accordingly. The retelling of the events that unfolded to ultimately cause the death of Elizabeth Roberts on the 15th July gave rise to a comment being made in the 27th July 1907 issue of the 'Rhondda Leader' by the reporter on the case, "The whole story showed a pitiful state of social life amongst some of the people in the Rhondda."

At the end of the proceedings at Ystrad magistrates court the prisoner, Thomas Edwards, was cautioned after which he declined to make a statement. Edwards was then formally charged and he was committed to take trial at the next Glamorgan assizes on a capital charge.

On November 8th 1907 Thomas Edwards's trial took place. The verdict returned by the jury found the accused man "Guilty of manslaughter." In delivering sentence against Thomas Edwards, Justice Sutton the presiding judge took into consideration the fact that Edwards had already served four months and sentenced him to a further period of imprisonment for eight months.

THE BROTHERS FATAL QUARREL WILLIAMSTOWN 1909

In communities like those that span the valleys, families are renowned not just for their communal spirit but for their closeness within the family unit. This can be even more apparent in times of crisis. The family unity was especially strong during the earlier years of the twentieth century, when the mining industry was working at full production and disasters were common occurrences which were prone to leave families grieving for another casualty.

In 1909 the strength of the family was as in previous years promoted by the chapels, in order that families could be afforded a greater chance to prosper in the hard working conditions and poor standards of living that they had.

The following case therefore has to be considered one of the more tragic cases to be recorded, especially so for the year 1909, when events like the case about to be described had to be for the time, a rare occurrence indeed.

Up until Wednesday April 21st 1909 the Young family who lived at 8 Brook Street, Williamstown enjoyed a reputation of respectability which also extended to the children of the family. The family consisted of Mr and Mrs Charles Young and their two sons George aged 17 and Sidney aged 15. The two boys were opposites in personality. Sidney was described as having a rather wild nature, while his brother George was considered to be delicate and of a quiet disposition. Despite their personality differences the brothers were thought to get on with each other quite well. Both brothers worked as collier boys at the Cambrian pit in Clydach Vale.

George, the elder and more sensible of the two boys, along with their parents were around the time of April 1907 concerned about Sidney's wild ways. They were also concerned about the company that he had taken to keeping.

Perhaps it was because of the company that Sidney was with, that an argument began between the two brothers at about ten past nine on the 21st of April in Penygraig Road.

George was enjoying an evening out with his friends when he saw his brother Sidney and for some reason ordered him to go home. Sidney probably protested against his brothers order and an argument broke out between the two boys. Sidney threatened his brother with a penknife, and as a result of the threat a scuffle ensued between them.

George may or may not have seen the penknife that his brother threatened him with. If he had seen it maybe he did not believe that his own brother would use the penknife. However, just a few moments into the scuffle George moaned deeply as Sidney thrust the knife into his brother's chest piercing his heart. Immediately after stabbing his brother Sidney ran away.

At the same time a little further down the road a woman by the name of Mrs Baker, although she was some distance from where the brothers were, heard George groan and turned around just in time to see him collapse to the ground. Mrs Baker ran to assist George and held him in her arms until another lady (a Mrs Adams) arrived on the scene. The two women were profoundly shocked to see blood oozing from a wound in George's chest.

While the women were trying to assist the mortally wounded lad, his condition worsened drastically and George Young lapsed into unconsciousness. As quickly as possible the ill-fated youth was carried to his home nearby. His anxious parents sent for a doctor, but before medical help arrived George succumbed to his injury and died.

When Dr. Watkins arrived he certified death and made an examination of the dead youth. He found a small incised wound above the heart, which in his opinion had been inflicted by a small penknife or similar and that the heart had been penetrated. The parents of George Young, upon realising how their son had died and whose hand caused his death, immediately were overcome with the most harrowing grief to be witnessed by those present.

The police were duly informed of the terrible events that had occurred. Immediately a search of the area was made for Sidney, who had been missing since running away after he had stabbed his brother. Policemen were posted throughout various points of the district to prevent Sidney from leaving the area. The search lasted until midnight when Sidney was found hiding at Ely pit, by the coke ovens on the mountainside at Penygraig.

Sidney was immediately arrested and taken to Tonypandy police station, where he was duly charged on the capital offence of the wilful murder of his brother. The knife used by Sidney to kill George, although initially searched for, was never recovered as Sindey had disposed of it by throwing it into the coke ovens.

On Friday the 23rd of April, the enquiry into the circumstances surrounding the death of George Young took place. The district coroner Mr. D. Rees conducted the enquiry. Deputy Chief Constable Cole and Inspector Hole of Tonypandy represented the police and the prisoner himself was not legally represented. The evidence given by those witnesses who attended the enquiry was considered to be amazing and of a contradictory character. The jury in respect of the evidence of at least one witness felt that the witness had been 'got at'. After much thought, the jury returned a verdict of "Manslaughter", with a recommendation for mercy on the grounds of his youth and also for the fact that the jury felt the act was committed under extreme provocation this being that his brother started the argument and instigated the scuffle that occurred between the two brothers.

On Monday the 26th of April the case against Sidney Young was heard at the juvenile court in Ton-Pentre. Despite the mass of people trying to gain entry into the building to view the proceedings, only those directly involved in the case were allowed entry into the courtroom.

Mr W.P. Nicholas, acting on behalf of the Crown, outlined the details of the tragic scenario of the 21st April after stating "It was his painful duty, on behalf of the Crown, to prosecute the youth, Sidney Young, on the charge of capital murder."

One by one witnesses were called to give their version of events which was to a certain degree conflicting to say the least. Mr W.P. Nicholas offered, following the evidence given, his opinion that Sidney Young be committed to trial on the charge of capital murder. Mr Nicholas then handed papers to the bench.

The papers were copies of a new Act of Parliament, which prevented the extreme penalty of the law being carried out on a youth. This meant that minors could no longer be sentenced to the death penalty, if found guilty on the offence of capital murder. Sidney Young was the first youth to be tried under this new Act of Parliament.

The court after much consultation and last-minute argument made their decision. Sidney Young was guilty of the manslaughter of his brother

George, but not guilty of murder. It was considered that the victim, George Young, had been the aggressor and Sidney had defended himself with the penknife. It was concluded that the two brothers had been in an everyday quarrel, during which Sidney lost his temper and produced the small penknife, which he then stabbed George with. It was stated by Mr Harold Lloyd, Sidney's defence lawyer, that in ninety-nine out of a hundred cases George would probably have sustained only a flesh wound. It was unfortunate that in this case the wound had proved to be one of a fatal nature. Sidney Young was committed to take his trial on the charge of manslaughter at the assizes. Sidney, still aged 15, stood trial on July the 21st 1909 three months after he had killed his brother.

Standing in the dock at the Glamorgan assizes in Swansea, before Mr Justice Sutton, Sidney Young pleaded guilty to the charge of manslaughter.

Mr B. Francis Williams, defence, asked the court for mercy on behalf of the youth who stood before them. Mr Williams stated that prior to the day of George's untimely death, the two brothers had enjoyed quite a good relationship and it had not been Sidney's intention to kill his older brother.

The plea for mercy did not fall onto deaf ears in the courtroom. Despite the fact that the youth was technically guilty of manslaughter, the judge felt that with consideration to his youth, Sidney had not meant his brother any great harm and felt that the boy may have even killed his brother by accident. The judge felt that no great degree of culpability could be attached to Sidney Young. The judge accepted that the deceased had been the aggressor in this case. The judge, finding no justification to send Sidney to prison, bound the youth over to come up for judgement if required before discharging him. Sidney Young then left the dock.

A FATAL GAME OF FOOTBALL WATTSTOWN 1912

On the 28th of March 1912, at Porth police court, Edwin George Hansford fell foul of the law when he appeared on a charge of having caused the death of William Edward Williams. The charge was brought due to Edwin George Hansford striking William Edward Williams, a very well-known Rhondda referee. Hansford allegedly struck Williams on the forehead with his fist, at the Butchers Arms in Wattstown on the 17th of February 1912.

It seems that events leading up to Edwin George Hansford being in the dock on the charges mentioned, began at a football match that was taking place on the 17th of February. Edwin George Hansford, a footballer for Wattstown, was playing with his team against Aberaman. William Edward Williams, who was by all accounts was considered to be "an exceptionally cool and quiet referee" was that day refereeing the match being played.

The game began normally enough and continued well until near the end of the match a dispute arose between Hansford and the linesman which necessitated William Edward Williams to interfere in order that the match could continue, which it did resulting in a win for the Aberaman team.

After the match, the players went into the Butcher's Arms to bathe and change. It was during this time that an argument broke out between the accused Hansford and William Edward Williams.

During the argument Hansford punched Williams in the right eye, causing his head to be knocked violently backwards. Williams then bent forward and covered his face. William Edward Williams felt ill from the blow he had received, causing enough concern for some of the players to take him to the surgery.

Dr. John Lyons found that Williams had a gash of about three quarters of an inch above his eye, which he dressed by placing a bandage around Williams's head. At that time, the doctor was not unduly concerned about the injury, which he was under the impression would heal within a short space of time.

William Edward Williams, still feeling unwell, saw the doctor again the next day (the Sunday).This time he saw Dr. William Henry Curtis. Again the doctor was not unduly concerned by Williams's injury. However William Edward Williams did not recover from the blow he received from Hansford and less than a month later on the 15th March 1912, William, aged just twenty-nine years, died.

A post-mortem examination was carried out on Williams. This was attended by Dr. Percy Clifton Peace of Tylorstown, who later testified that in his opinion William Edward Williams was found to have had a thickening of the fluid at the base of the skull, this he believed had been brought on by tubercular meningitis. The blow to his eye the previous month, Dr. Peace insisted, had been instigational in the condition arising which resulted in the death of Williams.

Apart from the thickening of fluid about the base of the skull, there were no other injuries to be found. Williams's organs were healthy. The only other point to be made by the doctor was that Williams's skull was exceptionally thinner than a normal skull would be.

The judge at the trial concluded that Edwin Hansford was guilty of manslaughter. The judge, however, applied leniency to Hansford under the circumstances of the case. Taking into consideration the fact that Edwin Hansford had been in prison since March, having served four and a half months, the judge sentenced him for a further one month of hard labour.

PENYGRAIG TRAGEDY

According to the local paper, the tragedy that was enacted on the night of Monday the 16th of October 1922 had 'all the elements of a grim drama.'

The murder itself took place in the small cosy kitchen of number one Nantgwyn Street Penygraig. There were a few occupants in the house on that night. The lodgers Mr and Mrs Jones were in the front room . Another lodger Benjamin James was in another room. In the kitchen sat Mrs Ella Margaret Berry, also known as Mrs. Nellie Francis. Also present were Ella's friend, Mary Ellen Thomas and another lodger, Harry Hill, who was on intimate terms with Mrs Berry, although he was seventeen years her junior.

The relationship between Harry Hill and Mrs Berry had not been going too well of late. Since the Thursday before matters had deteriorated further after Harry had been out drinking and an argument had arisen when Harry was to declare that he had said a number of things to Mrs Berry that he afterwards regretted. It seems that although Harry was still very fond of Mrs Berry, her affections for him had died. Earlier on the day of the 16th of October the affair and its difficulties had affected Harry greatly and at one point Mrs Berry's friend had found him in tears, but although he had tried his utmost to regain her interest it was all to no avail.

The scene that evening seemed on the surface to be very intimate, the three of them sitting cosily around the kitchen fire. Mrs Berry was reading aloud to her friend Mary Thomas while Harry quietly listened. Harry, still trying to gain Mrs Berry's attentions, asked her to accompany him outside, but she refused so Harry went out on his own to get some stout. Soon after Mary Thomas went out to buy It soon became apparent that Harry's emotions were still running high, especially when Mrs Berry further refused his offers of friendship. Something snapped in Harry's mind and he sprung out of his seat, grabbed Mrs Berry by the neck and with the words "Now I'll do for you!" proceeded to slit her throat. Mrs Thomas, speechless, looked on at the horrifying scene that was occurring in front of her. All Mrs Thomas could suddenly see was the blood that poured from the throat of her friend.

In a desperate struggle, the couple staggered to the room where Mr and Mrs Jones were staying. The Joneses having heard a noise thought that Mrs Berry's daughter Irene had fallen downstairs. But upon opening the door, they were amazed to see Ella Berry fall towards them clutching desperately for Mrs Jones's pinafore in an effort to try and quench the flow of blood from her throat. Mr Jones rushed forward to stop Harry from entering the room while Mrs Jones, with great presence of mind under the circumstances, slammed the door and then proceeded to barricade it with a carpet to stop Harry from entering. Ella Berry by now lay on the floor drenched in a pool of her own blood, still with the pinafore which Mrs Jones had used as a bandage wrapped around her neck. It was there on the floor that her life faded away.

Harry by this time had been forced into the kitchen by Mr Jones, Ben James and a neighbour William Griffiths who had rushed to the scene. As luck would have it a local policeman P.C. West, who had been on duty in the area at the time, was summoned and managed to secure Harry with handcuffs after quite a struggle. Shocked and dazed, Harry Hill remained seated and manacled in the kitchen amidst the great disorder that had been created by the struggle. He appeared unable to comprehend the significance of his actions. It was as if he existed in a world apart and he sat a broken and pathetic individual. Harry Hill made no protest as he was quietly led away by P.C. West to Tonypandy police station.

The shock and disbelief had affected the witnesses of the crime to such an extent that at the enquiry, which was held at Tonypandy library the following Thursday, there was little fresh evidence and great difficulty in discovering the real motive for the crime.

It seems that 49 year old Agnes Ellen Berry had been a woman of some refinement and had kept very much to herself, not being on close terms with any one of her neighbours. Because of this, neighbours statements concerning her were confused and lacking in any definition. But it did appear that she had had a somewhat complicated personal life. She was married to a Mr. Allen Parkman Berry, who was a painter and decorator, but she had lived apart from him for several years. No-one at this time knew of his whereabouts, although it later transpired that he was living in Cwmfelinfach.

For some time Mrs. Berry had lived at number one Nantgwyn street with a Mr. Francis, whose name she assumed. It had generally been regarded that he was her husband although he had died about a year before. Ellen Berry had borne two children, a boy aged 15 and a girl, Irene, who was 10 years old. Ellen Berry it was established had been on intimate terms with Harry Hill, who was one of her lodgers, for about six weeks.

Throughout the enquiry Harry Hill sat dejected and quiet between two constables. Harry was described as being a tall fair haired man with eyes of a brownish colour which bore 'a very peculiar vacant expression.' It was also noted with regard to his personal demeanour that ' a constant violent twitching of his body indicated the intense nervous strain that he was subject to.' A verdict of 'wilful murder' was returned and Harry Hill was taken out to a waiting car, which drove rapidly away due to the worry over a large crowd that had gathered outside the library in the hope of catching a glimpse of the accused man. However there was no demonstration and Harry Hill was removed to Cardiff gaol to await his trial.

Although in life she had kept very much to herself, great public interest was shown at Mrs. Berry's funeral, which took place on the following Friday at Trealaw cemetery. A number of wreaths covered the coffin and the roads around Penygraig were lined with crowds of people.

Harry Hill though was not without his sympathisers, and in order to secure a good defence the Rhondda branch of the British Legion stepped in and started an appeal aimed at ex-servicemen and the general public in order to raise funds. It seems that Harry's family who lived in London were not in any financial position to provide the funds themselves, but as Harry was an ex-serviceman they knew that support would be guaranteed from that quarter. Indeed, it was to be the effects of Harry Hill's war experiences that would ultimately save him, at least from the gallows.

It had been noted by the police, when the case came before the stipendiary, that Hill's condition seemed to be unstable. Because of this he had not been charged until the Wednesday, 'owing to his condition physically and mentally' and would therefore not have understood the charge had it been made.

At each appearance in court Hill displayed signs of acute nervousness and an uncontrollable twitching of the body.

Another piece of evidence that came to light was the discovery in Hill's pockets, amongst the razor and the war medals, of a number of letters written by the accused and one of which was signed 'The mad patient from Chepstow' and contained the sentence ' My brain is turned by the war and I have gone off my head.' Harry Hill was also to accuse Ella Berry of taking all that he possessed to the extent that he even had to pawn his clothes in order to give her money. Indeed evidence of the pawn tickets was found in his pockets.

At his trial at Swansea assizes, a little more of Harry Hill's history surfaced and a little more sympathy was gained for his defence, which was to be a plea on the grounds of insanity.

Although there was no doubt that Harry Hill had killed Agnes Ellen Berry by slitting her throat, the real question and outcome lay in deciding what the mental state of the prisoner was at the time of the murder. It transpired during the hearing that Harry Hill had been in the Naval Brigade and on the 8th of August 1918 he had been wounded and blown up resulting in him suffering from severe shell shock. Whilst he was on the stretcher after being wounded, he was hit again by a shell and buried in a dug-out. Hill was discharged from service on the 14th of December 1918 as a result of shell-shock and injuries suffered. In 1921 he had to give up work because of his condition. From that point there followed frequent admissions to the Ministry of Pensions Nerve Hospital at Chepstow, where he was found to be suffering from neurasthenia. Harry Hill also complained of headaches, insomnia, bad dreams and had developed a fear of darkness, of being alone and also hallucinations.

Dr David William Adreus had treated Harry Hill at Chepstow and declared, when cross-examined, that in his opinion 'It was possible for a person in a similar state of mind to that of the prisoner to have a frenzy and forget about it. It was also possible for a man who had received injuries to the head to develop insanity some years later.' Hill's mother, Clara Jessie Hill, was also called to the witness stand and was to declare that Harry had lived with her until he was about twelve years old. When he was young, she remembered he had fallen and sustained a concussion. She also stated that her own father had died in an asylum and there was also another case of insanity in the family.

The jury, after an hour's deliberation, returned a verdict of 'Guilty but insane.' His Lordship in passing sentence said 'that the prisoner shall be detained during his Majesty's pleasure.'

Insanity verdicts were not usually found outside murder cases where the possibility of a lifetime's confinement in a secure hospital was far worse than the punishment for the crime. For Harry Hill though, hospital confinement was certainly preferable to the hangman's noose.

Interestingly, with regard to the history of 'insanity defences', on the 20th of January 1843 a Mr Daniel McNaughten attempted to assassinate the then prime minister, Sir Robert Peel. But being unfamiliar with the exact appearance of Sir Robert, he shot his secretary instead. At the trial, the jury returned a verdict of 'Guilty but insane' and McNaughten was confined to a hospital.

However, such was the seriousness of the case and also the certain self interest to Parliament and public outcry at the verdict, that laws were passed that would determine that judges in the future, when trying insanity cases, should be guided by certain rules regarding insanity. These were to be known as the McNaughten Rules. However, with the advance in medicine in future years and the increasing advances in discoveries regarding the human brain and psychology, the rules began to be seen as rather oversimplified and reforms were deemed to be necessary to them. It was not until 1957 that parliament eventually took action and passed the Homicide Act of 1957 which allowed for the defence of 'Diminished Responsibility.'

UNTIMELY DEATH IN TREHERBERT

Christmas, traditionally a time of happiness, of family gatherings and excited children is not such a time for everyone. To some it can be a time when their problems are enhanced, a time of depression, a time when their loneliness is brought to the fore.

Perhaps it was some of these problems that pushed Rees Morgan Thomas beyond the brink of sanity and caused him to murder his 24 year-old sister-in-law Dorothy Irene Thomas on the morning of the 20th of December 1926. Rees, a 41 year old discharged soldier, lived with his brother Thomas Henry Thomas, his sister-in-law Dorothy, their twelve month old baby and his father at 98 Gwendoline Street, Treherbert.

According to Thomas Henry, there had never been any trouble or animosity between his wife and brother before, which was what made the tragedy that much more shocking. To all concerned, Rees Morgan's behaviour was totally unexpected, unprovoked and unexplainable, even to Rees himself it seemed.

On the early morning of the 20th of December 1926, P.C. Hill received a call at the police station and in consequence of the call he went to 98 Gwendoline Street, where he found the house to be in great disorder. The kitchen, where the murder took place, had broken glass strewn over the floor, pictures were broken and furniture had been thrown about the room. Mrs Dorothy Irene Thomas lay on the floor unconscious and was being attended by a Dr. Williams. P.C Hill found Rees, who was out in the back yard, in a 'frenzied state and very excited.' From what he was told it seems that Rees had attacked Dorothy and beaten her about the head with a flat iron.

Indeed, the murder was to become known by locals as the 'Treherbert flat iron tragedy.' P.C. Hill subsequently arrested Rees and charged him with causing Dorothy grievous bodily harm.

However, when Dorothy died the next morning in the hospital, the charge was changed to one of murder.

The shock that was felt among the local inhabitants of Treherbert was portrayed at the funeral of Dorothy. Thousands of people lined the streets leading to Treorchy cemetery where Dorothy was to be buried.

At the Glamorgan assizes in the following February, the trial of Rees was to come to a 'dramatic end.' His physical and mental condition was so bad by then that he had to be assisted into the dock. In consequence of this, Mr J.E. Arnold James who defended Rees stated that he had a submission to make 'That the accused was insane and therefore unfit to plead.' The medical evidence of a Dr. Fitzroy Jarrett, the medical officer at Cardiff prison, corroborated this. As a result the judge ordered that Rees be 'detained in strict custody until his Majesty's pleasure in regard to him is known.'

Rees Morgan Thomas was subsequently committed to Broadmoor asylum, where he was expected to stay indefinitely. However as events turned out Rees's time there was to be short, as on the 5th of March 1927, it was reported in the local paper that Rees had died in Broadmoor.

Rees had been a chronic epileptic and his health had been poor for a considerable time. The news of his death therefore came as no great surprise to those who knew him.

PORTH DOUBLE TRAGEDY

Porth, the village that many regard as being the gateway into the Rhondda valley, was the scene of a double tragedy in December of 1929.

On Sunday December the 29th, the bodies of Mr Thomas James Williams and his son Wilfred, who was just twenty four years old, were found at their combined home and business at 41 High Street Cymmer Porth. The two men had died as a result of throat wounds. No police search was instigated for the person responsible for this horrible deed, as the police had a witness.

The witness was Mr Thomas Williams's niece, Jessie Oliver. Jessie had been living and working at the shop for about twelve months, having moved in after the break-up of her marriage.

At the time of the double murder Jessie had been in the kitchen washing dishes at the sink.

Jessie Oliver was to testify that the day had started as any normal Sunday morning. Thomas Williams had arisen at about nine thirty and had come down for his breakfast. His son Wilfred got up a little later. Wilfred came downstairs as his father was shaving with a razor in front of a mirror that was hanging on the wall in the kitchen. Very few words besides "Good morning" were exchanged between them all, but this apparently was not unusual as Thomas Williams was not known to be very talkative in the morning.

Then quite suddenly and without any warning Thomas Williams rushed at his son with the razor and slit his throat. There had been no disagreement, in fact not a word from either of them had been said to cause such an action. As Wilfred lay dying under the kitchen table Jessie ran to her aunt, who was still upstairs, for assistance. But by the time Jessie and her aunt came down to the kitchen Thomas Williams had turned the razor on himself and he also lay dying on the floor.

That Thomas James Williams should act in such a way greatly surprised the local inhabitants of Porth. Until the time of his death he had always been a steady and upstanding character, having lived in Porth for over twenty years with his own business in the High Street as the local butcher. He was also active in local church circles, being a warden for St Peter's

St. Lukes. Porth

parish, superintendent of the Sunday school and also a lay preacher. Thomas Williams had also assisted in conducting the services at St. Lukes. Since the March before his death he had become a member of the Rhondda Council, having successfully stood as a Ratepayers candidate.

Thomas Williams's uncharacteristic actions, apart from surprising the local community also stunned his own family, in particular his brother John Williams from Cardiff. He had visited Thomas a fortnight earlier and although he found his brother to be low-spirited and depressed, with a feeling that everything was "crushing him down", John stated that he felt at the time that his brother was not one to have committed such a crime, despite having been unwell for the past six to nine months prior to the murder suicide.

As for committing suicide, John professed that Thomas '... was the last person in the world that you would expect to do that.'

It was to be a very distressing case for the jury at the inquest and they expressed much sympathy with the family of Thomas Williams. Not only did they have to suffer the feelings of confusion and bewilderment that surrounded the tragedy, but to suffer it under the glare of the publicity that the case attracted must have been even more distressing for them. The jury were not long in reaching a unanimous verdict to the effect that 'The son died as a result of the wounds that were inflicted by the father, and that the father was not in a mental state to appreciate what he was doing.' The jury did not consider it to be murder in any sense. This verdict must have come as some relief to the family who already had so much to deal with.

The funeral of both the father and his son witnessed some impressive scenes. The internment was in Trealaw and the route to the cemetery was lined with crowds of people. In some places they were lined four or five deep, with many representatives from the local council among the graveside mourners.

FERNDALE'S TRIPLE TRAGEDY 1935

When a person commits suicide, it is hard to imagine what it is that is going through their minds at the time they decide to commit the act of suicide. Do they suddenly wake up one morning and decide this is it feeling unable to go on any longer, or are some suicides spontaneous in their actions, suddenly snapping to find themselves overcome with an overwhelming urge to end it all? There are those who take their own lives and enquiries into their affairs have proved fruitless in finding any particular reason as to why the particular person felt that they had to end their life, whereas others are found to be bogged down with nightmarish problems.

What is hard to deal with is when a person decides to commit the act of suicide, but before they do other lives are ended or put into severe jeopardy by the intended suicide victim.

Could it be the case that for even a small reason, insignificant to you or me, a person can suddenly fly into a frenzy and kill others before then turning their own hand upon themselves ?

In recent years it seems that the suicide rate has increased in the Rhondda valleys, more so amongst the male population. Occasionally we hear in the news that a murder suicide has occurred within the confines of our valleys, however sadly more and more often these days we hear of a family member suddenly killing their spouse and children before turning a weapon on themselves and committing suicide. This scenario thankfully is not common but it is a more regularly heard-of event these days I am sad to say.

In 1935 murder suicides were quite a rare occurrence, so when one occurred in Ferndale the community were very grieved and shocked to hear of the tragedy that undoubtedly touched upon the lives of those who lived in such a close-knit community.

On the 31st of August 1935, Edward Edwards called at his daughter's house at 46 Duffryn Street Ferndale, at the request of his grandson Cyril. The time was 7.15 a.m. Upon entering the kitchen area of the house Mr Edwards was shocked to find his grand-daughter Phyllis Easterbrook bleeding profusely from wounds to her head. One of the two wounds she had to her head was quite a deep wound.

Edward Edwards immediately became deeply concerned by the sight of Phyllis, despite this his thoughts turned also to the welfare of the rest of his family. Edward Edwards began to search the rest of the house.

It surely must be impossible to imagine how the poor man felt when he entered one of the upstairs bedrooms and found his daughter Edith May Easterbrook (aged 38), his grand-daughter Joan (aged 8) and his 40 year old son-in-law of twenty years, Henry, all lying dead from horrific wounds that had been inflicted by a razor.

All evidence pointed to Henry Easterbrook as being the person responsible for the horrific scene that Edward Edwards had suffered the misfortune of having to witness.

At the inquest that took place on Monday 2nd September 1935, at which Mr R. J. Rhys coroner sat with a jury, it was revealed that Henry Easterbrook had five weeks prior to the day of the tragic find become unemployed. Despite his unemployment Henry did not seem to be troubled at the loss of work. Henry Easterbrook was by all accounts known to be a quiet man. Easterbrook was not known to be the type of person who had a quick temper and in fact he, his wife and family gave every appearance of being a happy and contented family who were of a close nature. There was and never had been until the 31st of August any trouble or bother of any sort.

Could the family possibly survive unemployment? After all we must remember that in 1935 there was no welfare system as such. Being unemployed and poor then in comparison to today is and was two very different kinds of reality. There is only a small percentage of the population today who truly know what 'poor' and 'poverty stricken' really means.

In the eyes of the outside world Henry Easterbrook may have been a man who suddenly and unexplainably reached into the depths of insanity on that fateful day, yet in his mind his irrational behaviour may to him have been considered to be a matter of logic and practicality.

Despite his madness, his actions may have been a display of love, no matter how wrong that seems to be to those of us on the outside looking in. However we shall never know the truth as to what it was that triggered the behaviour of Henry on that day in August of 1935. All that I can add is that each and every one of us has a breaking point, even seemingly happy and mild-mannered people of the gentlest dispositions have their breaking points. For some to reach that point it can take longer than others. Many thankfully never receive that final 'straw that broke the camels back', sadly though for Henry Easterbrook and his family he reached that point on that fateful day.

ROYAL CLEMENCY FOR A WATTSTOWN SOLDIER 1935

Although this case did not occur in the Rhondda area, the accused man came from Wattstown and as a result of this we felt that his story should be included in this book.

Arthur Charles Mortimer, aged 27 and a native of Wattstown, found himself in the dock of the Winchester assizes late in November of 1935. He stood accused of murdering a Miss Phyllis Oakes on the prior August 10th. The charge was that Arthur Mortimer had deliberately knocked Miss Oakes of her bike, whilst driving his car.

Mortimer, a soldier, was based at Aldershot and lived outside the barracks with his wife in married quarters.

The case opened with Arthur Mortimer pleading not guilty to the charges that had been brought against him. It was stated that although Phyllis Oakes died on the 10th of August, the prosecution were concerned with the events that related to the 8th of August when Phyllis Oakes and her sister Betty were cycling from Hardly Row in the direction of Oldham, when according to the evidence given by the surviving sister, Betty, she and Phyllis were cycling towards the railway bridge which crossed the Southern Railway. Betty stated that she and her sister were approaching the railway, where the road forks, when their way was nearly blocked by a big black saloon car. At this point the sisters were riding side by side, but broke into single file with Phyllis the deceased sister riding behind Betty. A train was passing underneath the bridge, drowning greatly the sound of a car that was approaching them from behind. To Betty's horror, moments later the car passed her and her sister was being carried on the bonnet of the car.

As the car passed over the bridge, Phyllis along with broken bits of her bicycle fell off the bonnet of the car which then disappeared from view.

Another witness, a Mrs Dobbie ran to get help for the injured woman. In answer to the witness's evidence, the defence for Arthur Mortimer argued that there had been an entire lack of intention on Mortimer's behalf to kill Phyllis Oakes, who succumbed to her injuries two days later on the 10th of August. The defence declared that Mortimer had mental health problems and had previously been confined to a mental health institution, and when he was released it was on the basis that his condition was relieved, not cured.

The defence asked that Mortimer be returned to an institution in order to have the help that he needed, at the same time he would if institutionalised be no longer a danger to the public at large.

Arthur Mortimer's doctor, David Henry Davies of The Poplars in Ynyshir, testified that as a youth Mortimer had problems. At the age of eleven and at the age of fifteen, the doctor had diagnosed Mortimer as being an epileptic. At seventeen, Dr. Davies had certified Mortimer as being of unsound mind, believing that at the time the accused was totally insane. This diagnosis was made on the basis that Dr. Davies had seen Mortimer in an extremely violent state and it had been drawn to his attention that on at least three prior occasions Mortimer had made violent attacks on women.

Despite this evidence given by Dr. Davies, the jury returned a verdict of 'Guilty of murder'. The Judge donned his black cap and passed the death sentence on Arthur Mortimer.

In January of 1936 Mortimer appealed against his death sentence. The unusual case of Mortimer deliberately running down a woman the day before her twenty-first birthday won no support for Mortimer and his appeal was rejected by the court.

Arthur Charles Mortimer appealed again, this time to Sir John Simon the Home Secretary, who in turn asked the newly crowned King Edward VIII to exercise Royal clemency. Following a medical inquiry into the mind of Mortimer, His Majesty the King exercised the Royal clemency, which granted Mortimer a reprieve from the death sentence. However Mortimer's sentence did not get him into a mental health institution, instead his sentence was commuted to penal servitude for life.

HORRIFIC MURDER IN WATTSTOWN 1947

The following case was of such a horrific and brutal nature that not only did it make big headlines in the papers, but in order to solve it Scotland Yard was called in to investigate.

The Rhondda valley played host in the most terrible of circumstances to the famous detective, Superintendent Capstick of the Yard.

Capstick, known as Charlie Artful his nickname given by criminals, was known to be a policeman who always got his man. In his day Capstick was famous for his detection work and his case-solving abilities. Capstick was instrumental in solving the notorious Blackburn murder in 1948, when a four year old girl was taken from the Queen's Park Hospital in Blackburn. The child was raped and then murdered in the grounds of the hospital. Capstick took desperate steps in order to catch the killer of one so young and innocent. It was Capstick who took the lead in deciding to have the whole male population of Blackburn fingerprinted in an effort to match prints found at the scene of the crime. This course of action was a first in the history of crime detection and the process also proved the persistence of Capstick in catching his man.

Just a year before the Blackburn murder, a murder of such a terrible nature occurred in Wattstown that it not only shocked the immediate community but the whole of Wales.

On Saturday the 11th of October 1947, at about 8 p.m., Rachel Allen (known locally as Rachel the washerwoman) in her habitual manner entered the Butchers' Arms in Wattstown. The landlord Daniel Rees served Rachel a half pint of beer. Rachel's usual custom was to sit on the bench in the passage, where she would drink alone. Rachel Allen being a familiar figure about the hotel would often have drink bought for her by regulars who knew her.

On this particular evening 76 year old Rachel wandered over to the doorway of the singing room, where upon the invitation of the chairman she went in and sat at the rear of the room to watch the concert that was taking place. Sometime later during the evening Evan Haydn Evans entered the Butchers' Arms and was seen talking to Rachel before turning on her and insulting her with crude language.

It is not known what time Rachel left the Butchers' Arms, but she visited the local general store (situated near to the Butchers' Arms.) at 10 p.m. to buy her daily box of snuff and to ask for one sweet 'off the ration.' Doris Day the assistant who served Rachel noted the time as being 10.05 p.m. when Rachel left the store.

Rachel, who was presumed to be a widow when her husband failed to return from the Great War, headed for her home, 76B Hillside Terrace, or so the following events indicated.

Sometime between 10 p.m. and 10.30. p.m. Mrs Fricker, a neighbour living directly opposite Rachel, heard the old lady scream. She did not think to be concerned about hearing the scream as Rachel Allen loved cats which she kept. Many were passing strays that she would tend to. Often Rachel could he heard shrieking at the passing traffic if it drove too near to her beloved cats. Prior to Mrs Fricker hearing Rachel scream a truck had passed by.

The only other sighting of Rachel occurred sometime just after 10 p.m. when she was seen having an argument with a dark-haired man. Rachel was heard to shout at the man, 'If you don't go along, I will report you to the police.'

Although a popular and well-liked woman in the area, Rachel Allen was a recluse who preferred to live alone with her beloved cats. Even though Rachel lived in a four roomed house, she lived and slept in the kitchen. Rachel was in extremely poor circumstances, having just a pound to live on per week after her rent was paid. The only furnishings in Rachel's home comprised two chairs, a crudely-built table and an improvised bed. Despite living in such a state of poverty, Rachel fed her cats well with tins of sardines, foregoing her own rations to do so.

At 11.20 p.m. Mollie Morris, who lived next door to Rachel, returned from visiting her sister-in-law across the road. In order to get to her property Mrs. Morris had to enter through a communal door which led into a small yard that led respectively to the two women's own front doors. The yard was dark due to a high wall which prevented light from a near-by gas street lamp illuminating the yard.

As Mrs Morris entered the yard she 'stumbled over something.' Her first thoughts were that she had tripped over one of Rachel's many cats, even though the usual 'howl' of a cat being tripped over was not heard. Mrs

Morris entered her home and lit her gas lamp. Returning to the yard with the lamp, Mrs Morris was horrified to find that she had stumbled over the brutalised body of Rachel Allen. Mrs Morris ran screaming hysterically from the yard. Her brother-in-law, residing nearby, heard Mrs Morris's screams and quickly arrived on the scene to be greeted by the same sight.

The village was soon swarming with plain-clothed detectives and uniformed officers. The crime scene was immediately secured by the police and it was very quickly decided due to the apparent brutality of the crime that Scotland Yard be called in.

At 10 p.m. on Sunday evening, the day following the murder, Chief Detective Inspector Capstick accompanied by Detective Sergeant Stoneman arrived at the murder scene and with immediate effect took over the murder investigation.

Rachel Allen's body was viewed by Capstick. Her remains lay in a pool of blood. Terrible injuries to her face and head rendered her features virtually unrecognisable. Her clothes were in a state of disarray with her skirt pulled up to her waist. Rachel Allen's undergarments were torn, all indications were that she had been raped. Strangely, still clutched in her hand was her front door key. The tin of snuff that she had bought lay next to her mutilated body.

The whole of the crime scene was examined, the back door and the frame along with samples of blood were sent to a forensic labratory in Cardiff, while the defiled remains of Rachel Allen were taken to the mortuary at East Glamorgan Hospital for a post-mortem examination.

An extended search of the Wattstown area was made in an effort to find a possible murder weapon and any further clues that could lead the police to identify a savage killer. For three days a very frightened and shocked community was subjected to the questions of the police, who had no shortage of informants to help them with their enquiries.

On the Monday evening following the murder, an exited atmosphere of expectancy charged around police headquarters as rumours spread of an arrest being imminent. In the early hours of Tuesday the 14th, Capstick accompanied by other police officers arrived at 39 Heol Llechau, the home of twenty-one year old Evan Haydn Evans.

Evans, who was asleep, was soon woken by the police. Capstick duly informed him that they were police officers making enquiries into the murder of Rachel Allen. Evans was asked to explain where he was on the Saturday night in question, between the hours of 10.15 p.m. and 11.20 p.m. Evans replied that he did not do it and that he knew nothing about the murder, adding that after leaving the Butchers Arms he came straight home.

Whether or not it was informants' statements that led the police to Evan Haydn Evans's home is unsure, but once the police were there Evans's reaction to questioning aroused the suspicious instincts of the officers who were questioning him. Evans as a result was asked to accompany Capstick back to the police station which he agreed to do.

Evans dressed for his trip to the police station, but strangely refused to wear a pair of freshly-polished black shoes offered to him by his mother, opting in favour of a pair of brown shoes.

Evan Haydn Evans was taken back to Ferndale police station, where he was cautioned before being questioned. Evans was again asked where he was at the times previously asked. His answer was the same. When asked what clothes he wore on the previous Saturday, Evans claimed to be wearing the blue suit that he had on. When asked about shoes, Evans claimed not to remember what shoes he had been wearing.

The police, unknown to Evans (also known as Blackie John due to his very dark features) knew that he owned a dark brown suit and witness statements indicated that Evans had been wearing it on the night of the murder. Inspector Williams was sent to Evans's home to collect his black shoes and all clothing. Capstick told Evans that he was not satisfied with his answers and informed Evans that his clothes would be microscopically examined for traces of blood.

To this Evans sat thoughtfully for a few minutes before stating that he did remember after all what had happened, adding that after drinking eight to ten pints at the Butchers' Arms it was hard to recall events with great exactness. Evans then went on to state that he felt pretty drunk on the way home. He claimed to accidentally bump into the victim, Rachel Allen, who fell against a wall. Rachel was outside calling to her cats at the time. Evans then alleged that Rachel called him a filthy pig and threatened him with the police. At these remarks Evans lost his temper and hit Rachel through the communal door and into the small yard.

Evans's statement went on to say that he repeatedly punched the old woman, who fell onto the floor. Unrelenting in his attack Evans continued his onslaught by kicking the defenceless woman repeatedly in the face. Evans still not satisfied with his level of violence committed further insult to Rachel by then raping her. Before leaving the violated and horrifically beaten body of Rachel Allen Evans again kicked the lifeless woman. Before leaving the scene of his crime Evans lit a match and viewed the body of Rachel before going home. Evans stated that his mother was up when he arrived home and questioned him about being covered in blood. His answer was that he had been fighting. Evans mother was upset as the dark brown suit he was wearing was after all new on that very day. As a result of Evans's statement, he was formally charged with the murder of the harmless, popular old lady who had a great passion for her cats.

It was during the early part of December that Evan Haydn Evans's (Blackie John's) trial opened at the Cardiff assizes. During the course of the trial the extent of the horrific onslaught on Rachel Allen became fully apparent when the pathologist gave evidence to the court. Dr. C.R.E. Freezer stated that the post-mortem on Rachel Allen revealed many injuries to her body. There were numerous superficial wounds to the whole of the face. Bloodstains and smears on the inner thighs and the legs indicated that she had been raped. The bones of the victim's face were broken into a great many fragments. The skull was fractured as well as a few of her ribs. A matchstick was found shoved into the victim's nostril. Death was due to shock brought on by the horrific injuries inflicted upon her. Dr. Freezer also stated that before the time of the murder, Rachel Allen would have been a relatively fit woman.

It was suggested but not proved that the rape may have taken place after death as opposed to before death. If this was the case then Evans had committed necrophilia. This perversion brought on in all possibility through the presence and sight of seeing a dead body.

In defence of Evans, Mr Llewellyn Williams claimed psychological disturbances as a contributing factor in Evans's actions on the fateful night in question. It was also revealed that Evan Haydn Evans had suffered deep grief and distress as a result of his twin sister dying six months prior to the night of the murder.

Forensic examination revealed blood splatters all over the suit that Evans had been wearing.

Fragments of bone and brain tissue had also been found on the trousers that he had worn. Evans standing at just four feet eleven inches and very slimly built, was before the murder stated to be a quiet, unassuming and inoffensive young man who had followed his father into the mine.

Evans was up until the time of the murder a colliery turbine driver in one of the Trehafod pits (probably the Lewis Merthyr pit). Evans was the only boy in a family of four children and it seems that before her death he was terribly attached to his twin sister.

When Evans was questioned in the witness box, it became apparent that he probably did not realise the seriousness of his position. He could not explain what motive he had in committing the murder and in fact he stated that he did not know when he left Rachel Allen whether or not he had killed her. The answers given in the witness box by Evans reflected his uncaring and thoughtless attitude towards his victim at the time of her murder.

Another witness, a friend and workmate of Evans, stated in the witness box, that on the Monday following the murder the witness upon walking into work with Evans mentioned the murder.

During the conversation, Evans laughed off what had happened to Rachel Allen. The witness albeit at the time with no inclination of Evans's guilt, in jest warned Evan Haydn Evans to be careful in case the police came after him for the murder. Again Evans laughed the matter off.

The case for the prosecution concluded. The jury took only forty minutes to return with a verdict of 'Guilty of murder.' The judge donned his black cap and meted out the death sentence on the man who had so brutally murdered and raped Rachel Allen, a defenceless old woman who was fifty five years his senior.

During late January 1948 Evan Haydn Evans had an appeal heard at the court of criminal appeal, in the hope that he could have his charges reduced from murder to manslaughter in order to evade the death penalty. The appeal failed guaranteeing Evans his long walk to meet the short rope of justice.

The sentence was carried out on the third of February 1948 at Cardiff prison. On a rainsoaked morning at 9 a.m. the notice was pinned up on the gates informing those who had gathered outside that sentence had been carried out and that justice had been done.

EPILOGUE TO ADULT MURDERS

The cases so far covered in this book are cases dating up to the mid nineteen fifties it not being our intention to record murders after this period of time, however we could not conclude this section of the book without mentioning a recent murder that was committed in the locality and the tragic coincidence that was brought to our attention at the time of this murder.

On the 7th of September 1999 nineteen year old Richard 'Dikey' Davies, a well known local youth was found by the police at the junction of Queen Street and Victoria Street, Ton Pentre.

Richard was found to have suffered appalling head injuries. His injuries were so severe that he succumbed to them on or around the 9th of September 1999.

It later emerged that Richard Davies, who rented a flat at Glyndwr Court on Ystrad Road in Pentre, had in fact been in his flat when he was attacked and beaten with a dumbbell.

The police very quickly arrested two men in connection with the murder of Richard Davies.

Twenty six year old Darren Almond and Jason Gethin, also aged twenty six were charged with the murder of Richard Davies on the 11th of September. The two men appeared in court on the 12th and 13th of September respectively and were remanded into custody.

The two men came to trial in April 2000 and as a result Darren Almond was sentenced to five years in prison after being found guilty of grievous bodily harm with intent. Jason Gethin, who was at one time a representative for Wales as an international boxer, was jailed for life after being found guilty of Richard Davies's murder. At the time Jason Gethin committed the murder he was found to be an alcoholic and a hopeless junkie.

After Richard's murder, a strange quiet came over Pentre, usually busy with weekend drinkers visiting local pubs and clubs, Pentre held an eerie silence with noticeably fewer people being about on the streets. A lone

Glyndwr Court, just days after the brutal murder of Richard Davies. A lone policewoman guards the premises as the flats were put under forensic scrutiny for a number of days. (See prologue to adult murders.)

policeman stood at the entrance into the flats where Richard lived and flowers laid in sympathy and remembrance lined the pavement along the wall of the building where the victim had lived. The community had been stunned into silence from the shock of such a horrific crime occurring on their doorstep. The death of Richard Davies was another tragic and senseless act of violence and a terrible waste of a young life.

Another tragic aspect to this case is the awful coincidences that became apparent. Richard was murdered exactly ninety five years to the same week as Emlyn Jones in the Bridgend Hotel .

Both Emlyn Jones and Richard Davies's killers were charged on the 11th of September. On the 12th of September Emlyn Jones's killer appeared in court as did one of the participants in Richard's murder. Again on the 13th of September, there was another appearance in court for one of the men involved in Richard's death and on that same date ninety five years earlier the inquest into Emlyn Jones' death was held. Both murders were committed within a hundred and fifty yard distance of each other.

A marked difference between the two crimes was that at the time of the Bridgend Hotel murder crowds of people thronged the streets around the scene of the crime. The crowds were present for a few days or more, this being the reaction of horror and disbelief in 1904. As already stated the 1999 murder gave rise to the eerie silence that fell over the area. Perhaps a reflection of how differently we as a public react in the wake of tragedy?

We also noted during the course of our research that in a ninety seven year period, between 1902 and 1999, over a distance of less than a mile there had been no fewer than five murders committed in the Pentre area. This we felt may be an unusually high statistic, despite the span of time covered by these events. Three of these deaths occurring within a 200 yard radius.

All of these cases in turn were tragic. A death in the Woodfield Hotel, a murder in Volunteer Street; in the child murders chapter, a thirteen year old murdered by her mother in Treharne Street; the Bridgend Hotel murder and the Glyndwr Court murder. All tragic deaths, of which we the authors hope that the victims will at least be remembered kindly.

In conclusion, we hope that the chain has been broken and that Pentre at least will not be made to endure any more tragic and senseless murders.

Map showing a 1919 view of Pentre, where five murders have been committed. Marked on the map are the locations where each of the five murders took place.

A - Bridgend Hotel Murder 1904, page 31

B - A Fatal Affair in Pentre 1902, page 20 (Volunteer Street).

C - Death in the Woodfield Hotel, Pentre, page 16

D - Baileys Arms - Epiloque to Adult Murders, page 81

E - Pentre Child Murder 1949, Baglan Street, page 111

Old Coal Levels
680
6·539
682
2·324
Lle-tecca Cottages
Mission Room
Pentre
Catherine Street
Thomas Street
434a
·261
Reservoir
Sunday School
Pentre Collieries
Engine House
Shafts
Tramway
Brewery
Hotel
Picture Theatre
Shaft
Reservoir
712b
5·796
Spring
B.M. 546·7
Woodfield Hotel
Old Coal Level
Forge Street
Churchfield Row
Chap.
Wesley Place
Bank
Chapel
Pleasant View
School
Old Coal
715
19·980
Bailey Arms (P.H.)
Grand Theatre
Bridgend Hotel
B.M. 512·5
Club
Shay Street

INTRODUCTION TO CHILD MURDERS

It did not seem fair that we should write this book cataloguing murders in the valleys without devoting a section to the most vulnerable of victims that lived during the time frame that we have covered, those being the children.

The following cases are just a small example of the child related cases that appeared at the time.

Although they are not all murders or manslaughter cases, they are small examples of the dangers that children living at that time faced.

Some of the most vulnerable members of the family, other than women and the elderly, are children and the nineteenth century was riddled with such cases of child abuse and neglect. The nineteenth century especially was a dangerous time for children. Many infanticides were never brought to the attention of the magistrates and went unrecorded in the police courts, due to the fact that there was poor evidence as to whether the deaths were natural or due to neglect and violence.Child mortality was high anyway and public attitudes towards illegitimacy meant that many children born to unmarried mothers and servant girls were often smothered at birth and the babies' bodies hidden in the undergrowth, on tips, in boxes and attics. Other child murders were written off as stillbirths when there was little evidence to prove otherwise, at a time when mothers faced with yet another mouth to feed whilst living already under conditions of extreme poverty could find no other way out of their dilemma than to rid themselves of their newly born child. The Poor Law Amendment Act of 1834 saw a reduction in the help given to unmarried mothers and many babies were abandoned outside chapels or houses and often died as a result of this.

Most infanticides occurred therefore against children under one year old and murders of children over that age were rare though, as the local papers reflect, the instances of neglect, violence and cruelty to children remained high. But as David J.V. Jones has noted in his book, '*Crime in 19th Century Wales*' "*Children too received little sympathy against violence.*

The rulers of Victorian Britain were torn between the sacrilege of interfering with family life and legal patriarchy."

Crimes against children were largely under-reported and the punishment of the guilty parties was lower than with other crimes.

But apart from the murder cases, as can be seen by the cases reported in this book, violence towards children and neglect was statistically high. Much of the cause of this was the immense poverty and also alcohol abuse. Many of the cases of neglect and cruelty were alcohol related and both parents were often the guilty partners. Drunken fathers were violent to their offspring and drunken mothers were often neglectful and uncaring towards the children. Many children died as a result of their treatment, but such was the attitude of the magistrates of the time that the charge of manslaughter was rarely given through lack of evidence and a general apathy and detachment towards working class children.

As well as the dangers children faced from a poor upbringing there were also the general dangers of homelife. Children died from drinking whiskey left around the house, from drinking carbolic acid and other lethal substances. There are instances of children being burned to death as a result of unattended candles. Outside the home children faced dangers, being run over by carts or killed at the pits from playing near the machinery for example.

The N.S.P.C.C. and other reformers however, took the initiative and were paramount in helping to improve the lives of children, being responsible for the many prosecutions relating to child abuse and cruelty.

Although a depressing picture, ironically the high crime rate against children has helped to change the laws and people's attitudes also changed towards the end of the nineteenth century.

The passing of the Children's Acts of 1933, 1963, and 1969 meant that more children were given the help and protection they needed. The crimes against children have certainly reduced recently with the added protection and the ability of authorities to recognise more instances of neglect and cruelty and to deal with them accordingly.

However violence towards children remains an emotive issue and it is sad to think of how many children had to die, although the extent of the crimes before these changes were implemented will never truly be known.

TREHERBERT CHILD MURDER

Tynewydd, was described in the *Pontypridd Herald* on Saturday May the 26th 1894 as 'A village about a mile from Treherbert, in the Rhondda Valley. The population is essentially made up of colliers who work in the neighbouring pits.' Tynewyd was a village like many others in the valleys at the time where couples married and brought up large families in poor circumstances.

Life was hard, but the people knew no other way of living.

The married life of Mr and Mrs David Jenkins was similar to most. Their lives were of the usual uneventful character, which mark the better class of miners. Margaret Jenkins having been married for twenty one years, bore twelve children, six of whom died; uneventful perhaps in those days, but today her life would have been termed as being more tragic.

The working class mining valleys of the nineteenth century were no strangers to child mortality, but infanticide was something that could still shock the close-knit working class community of the Rhondda.

At three thirty in the afternoon of the 8th of May 1894, David Jenkins was awoken from his sleep by his wife Margaret who was calling him from downstairs. Still tired from having worked the night shift, David got up and went downstairs. They were a happily married couple who lived at numbert 9 Bryn Wyndham Terrace in Tynewydd although as with other mining families they had to face difficult times when colliery work was not always regular, and without work they had little or no food to eat. David Jenkins upon going downstairs was little prepared for the sight that faced him on that Friday afternoon.When he entered the room he saw his wife sitting quietly by the fire-side in an armchair, but the new baby, who was only seven weeks old, was no-where in sight.

When he inquired twice as to the baby's whereabouts, Margaret answered him in Welsh. Rwy wedi cwpa babi (I have finished the baby and it is in the pantry.) David went to the pantry and there saw on the salting stone table the result of Margaret's statement. On the table lay the headless corpse of Elizabeth Anne, his baby daughter. Her head was on the

Number 9 Bryn Wyndham Terrace, Tynewydd.

ground beneath and a bloodied axe lay on the floor beside it. Dazed and confused David left the house to fetch Police Constable T. Bryan, who on arriving, removed the remains to the kitchen table and wrapped them in a napkin. He charged Margaret with the wilful murder of her child, to which she confessed, "Yes I did it with the axe."

It transpired during the court case that Margaret had been a sufferer from what would now be termed post-natal depression. Indeed it had been reported in the the paper that; "It was noticed each time, before and after she was pregnant, Mrs Jenkins was the victim of considerable depression of spirits." So although such symptoms were recognised then, the treatment meted out to such sufferers was more in line with treatment given to the mentally insane. Indeed such illnesses were seen as forms of insanity as a Dr Llewellyn Powell was to attest in the witness box during the court case;

The coroner - "Is it not a fact that some women after confinements, when depressed, give way to a mania - puerperal mania?"

Dr Powell - "Yes, but the period of puerperal mania was past; but, if developed, it might keep on for six months. I should be disposed to believe that it would be a kind of lactation mania - during the suckling period. In those cases people got cruel too and are known to attack those they are most fond of."

At the Swansea assizes on Wednesday the 27th of June 1894, forty year old Margaret Jenkins was charged on two indictments, with feloniously and with malice aforethought killing and murdering one Elizabeth Anne Jenkins, her infant child, at Treherbert on the 18th of May 1894.

However, evidence was given as to her insanity at the time of the offence and the jury returned a verdict that she was unfit to plead due to this. The judge ordered her to be detained in custody pending Her Majesty's Pleasure. Margaret Jenkins was deemed to be 'Guilty but insane.'

The remains of little Elizabeth Anne Jenkins were buried at Treorchy Cemetery, where the chief mourners were her father and his six children.

NEGLECTED CHILDREN

The case of 'Neglected children' was one such instance where the hardships of working-class life in industrial South Wales and alcohol abuse were to be the prime causes of a colliers neglect and cruelty to his wife and four children.

The case was reported in the *Rhondda Leader* on the 10th of June 189 and concerned a Mr Thomas of Hopkinstown and was heard at Pontypridd police court before the stipendary, Mr Ignatius Williams.

Thomas was charged with neglecting his children whose ages ranged from twelve months to ten years the eldest two being his step-children. As with nearly all child cruelty cases it was voluntary organisations such as the N.S.P.C.C., who played a significant role during the 1890s when child cruelty cases rose sharply, by taking on the prosecution against Thomas.

The Victorian state at the time was reluctant to interfere to any great extent with family life and thought that it was from such 'violent' and 'lowlife' homes that the source of delinquency and crime arose. A Mr James Spickett prosecuted on behalf of the N.S.P.C.C. The case was described in the papers as "One of a most revolting character."

Mrs Thomas alleged that she received no money from her husband since the 9th of April and had been expected to survive on just eight and a halfpenny worth of food, which he himself had bought.

As a result of this the children suffered greatly from want of food while, she stated, Thomas himself spent all his time at the local public house.

On Whit-Monday, in desperation as the youngest child had become very ill, she gave it cold tea to drink having no money to buy milk, although the doctor on seeing the child had advised her to give brandy and milk.

James Spickett then stated that as a result of starvation the little child was not expected to live more than one day. The child itself, a girl, was found on being examined by Dr. Daley to weigh only 12lbs although in his estimation at thirteen months old its normal weight should have been about 21 lbs.

When faced with the charge of behaving cruelly to his family, Mr. Thomas's defence was that his "...wife was too dangerous for him to live with, and she always irritated him." At least his gaol sentence of three months with hard labour took him away from his source of irritation although I am sure he truly deserved a much longer sentence.

TREHERBERT CHILD'S DEATH

Another case of the death of a child through neglect and ignorance by the parent and again involving alcohol, although this time the child died as a direct result of drinking it, occurred in Treherbert in June 1899.

The case heard before Mr R.J. Rhys coroner, who seems to have presided over many of these inquiries, concerned the death of Mary Gwen Evans, the three year old daughter of William Evans, who worked as a hitcher. He lived with his wife and daughter at 37 Hopkin Street, Treherbert. It was alleged that the child had died on Monday morning as a direct result of drinking half a cup-full of raw whiskey that had been left by the father on the table when he went to get hot water to mix with it to give to his wife, who was ill upstairs in bed.

When he returned from the kitchen the cup was empty except for some sugar that was left in the bottom of the cup. Mary Gwen Evans continued to play with her doll for a further half an hour. Her father William, meanwhile, took no further action and just presumed that it was she who had drunk the whiskey. She later, not surprisingly, fell asleep for some time. It was later in the afternoon that he took her upstairs to continue her sleep and at 5 p.m. he noticed she was having a fit which prompted him to call in a neighbour and inform the local doctor.

Alcohol is absorbed from a person's stomach at about the rate of one unit an hour and is distributed around the body. For an adult inexperienced drinker, death could be caused after the intake of over 500mg of alcohol, about thirteen pints of beer. The effects of alcohol on a person varies greatly upon their experience of it, but its effects can also be affected by heat and cold, illness or disease, medication and how much food the person has eaten.

On being questioned by the coroner, William the father stated that other than sleeping, she seemed little affected by the alcohol, showing no signs of wandering at all. He stated that "He had previously seen her drink beer and porter. She was a strong child." On being asked by the coroner why he had not thought to call the doctor immediately after the child had drunk the whiskey. He replied, "I never thought, but that she had slept it out."

By a quarter to nine in the night when Dr. Grant arrived at the house the child was in a stupor and never regained consciousness. He applied a stomach pump and draught but by then only succeeded in drawing water from the stomach and could detect no traces of alcohol. By the following morning she had died. Alcohol poisoning was put as the reason for her death on the death certificate. Doctor Grant stated that, in his opinion, the child's life could have been saved if he had been called earlier.

William Evans was not charged with the neglect of his child, but received a 'severe censure' from the coroner who told him, "You are a very stupid man, if you had used your common sense your little girl might have been alive today. You have brought this trouble upon yourself."

Although not charged by the court, William had to live for the rest of his life with the realisation that it was through his neglect and stupidity that his daughter had died. A hard enough sentence in itself. There was no report that the couple had any other children at the time.

FERNDALE MANSLAUGHTER

It was the death of a ten week old baby girl at Ferndale on Monday the 28th of August 1899 that was to turn a charge of neglect to one of manslaughter against her mother Mary Withers of 106 Duffryn Street, Ferndale.

Mary Withers was twenty-five at the time and married to Frederick Withers. They had been married for seven years. The couple had only been living in Ferndale for about a week, having just moved there from Pontcanna in Cardiff. It would seem that the marriage, however, was not a harmonious one as the couple had been separated from each other for about twelve months.

Mary Withers had taken to drinking rather heavily and because of this and the problems in their marriage, Frederick had moved out and was now living at 24 Frederick Street, Ferndale.

Frederick had obviously kept in close contact and had been so worried about the health of his delicate ten week old daughter Mary Withers that on the Monday, a week before she died, he had sent a letter to Dr. Parry's surgery requesting that he see the child as a matter of urgency as he believed that she may be dying. On the Wednesday, Dr. Parry's assistant called at the house but could not gain admittance.

On Friday the 25th of August a large crowd had gathered outside 106 Duffryn Street and Frederick on seeing the disturbance went for the assistance of the local policeman P.C. Ryan, and together they forced open the front door. The scene before them was one of extreme neglect and disorder.

Except for a few crusts there was found to be no food in the house. Mary Withers, it seems, had spent from the 23rd to the 25th of August locked in the house drinking herself stupid. The evidence for this was the three dozen bottles of Anglo-Bavarian ale, 26 of which were empty.

Mary Withers "mad drunk" stood before them downstairs. She was dressed only in her night-dress with her hair hanging down her back. Suddenly they heard a faint cry coming from upstairs and when P.C Ryan

Ferndale Police Station

went up, he saw the baby May lying on an old mattress on the bed, the bed clothes being strewn about the floor. The baby was very weak and unkempt-looking and looked, by the dirt on her hands and face, as if she had not been washed for two or three days.

The child by now "... was very cold and had collapsed, it's little eyes were sunken and it was almost paralysed." Dr. Parry gave May to a neighbour, a Mrs Catherine James, of 110 Duffryn Street, who took the baby away to look after it.

Mary Withers meanwhile was taken to Pentre police station in a cab and was charged the following day with wilful neglect of her child.

Baby May, under the care of Mrs. James, seemed to have rallied a little by the Sunday, but it seemed that the extent of neglect that the child had suffered had been too much for a ten week old baby to endure and she died on Monday the 28th of August 1899.

An inquest into the death of the baby was held at Ferndale police station the following Wednesday by Mr. R.J. Rhys, coroner. The jury heard Dr. Parry's evidence to the effect that he did not believe that the baby had been systematically neglected. He did not see it as a delicate child, but small for its age weighing only ten pounds, but he did believe that the mother's neglect over those three days had accelerated her death. Because of this, the charge of neglect was changed to one of manslaughter against Mary Withers and she was removed to Cardiff gaol upon remand.

It would seem strange that nothing was said about the other children in the family, for from the little history recorded in the paper regarding the couple's past life, it appears that they had had five children together. Only one of these children had survived and this was a boy called Arthur, who was four years old. Of his whereabouts during these proceedings nothing is said and the whole affair leaves one wondering how these other children had met their deaths. Perhaps all were victims of neglect, but given the high rates of infant mortality in the 19th century it would seem that the magistrates thought it not worth bothering to enquire. It was a fact of life in those times.

It seems the sad case of a mother, unable to cope with motherhood and a troubled marriage, during difficult times, having found herself moved to the industrial valleys found her only comfort in drink. Having lost the will to take any responsibility for herself or her children all she could say in her defence when charged with manslaughter was, "It's so much my husband's fault as mine for bringing me to such a place."

Frederick Withers did not at first look as if he were to get away scot free and was later charged with the neglect of the child, the prosecution taken up by the N.S.P.C.C.. The charge being that as the child's father and knowing the state of affairs as regards his wife's alcoholism and child's illness he should have taken more responsibility and not absented himself from the house.

However when his wife was called to give evidence against him, at the advice of her solicitor she refused to do so and the charge was dropped. A sad affair concerning unhappy and vulnerable people, but as with many such cases the children ultimately pay the higher price.

CHILD NEGLECT AT MAERDY

A report that first appeared in the *Rhondda Leader* of the 16th of November 1901, clearly shows the extremes to which child neglect can be taken if not redressed in time. The report also shows the difficult living conditions that people were faced with in the industrial valleys and the kind of poverty they had to deal with on a daily basis. As usual it was the children who suffered having to accept in silence the world that their parents had brought them into.

In this case one can feel some sympathy for the father in having to face the difficult situation of raising two children, his own and his step-child, on his own after his wife had died.

The case in question concerned a William Howells, who was a thirty-two year old collier, who had recently moved into lodgings belonging to his landlady Mrs. Rachel Jones at 3 Rowley Terrace, Maerdy. Howells's wife had died just over a year before and he was therefore left to bring up two young children on his own. The elder was Mabel aged seven and the younger was Elizabeth Ann, aged three and a half.

William Howells had found it hard to get lodgings in Maerdy and having the two children made his effort to find lodgings all the more difficult. Due to the shortage of decent lodgings, Howells found himself at Rowley Terrace. The house had only three bedrooms which were being used by Rachel Jones to house twelve people, eight of them being adults. There was Rachel Jones, the landlady and her husband, another couple named Jones with their two young children, three male lodgers and now William Howells and his two young daughters. At that time this was a common state of affairs amongst the working classes. It was also not unusual for beds to be shared in a relay system, although it is amazing as to how detached the middle classes were from the realities of working class life. Later during the hearing of the case the judge, a Mr. Justice Kennedy was to comment upon hearing about the living arrangements, "I hope this sort of thing is unusual, this is a colliery district, is there that much overcrowding? Here we have a bad case, little children among all those

Number 3 Rowley Terrace, Mardy

grown up people in three little rooms."

However, the situation became too much for William Howells when he was expected to share a bed with two other adults, so he moved out to other lodgings. Howells left his two children behind when he moved. They were put under the care of the landlady Mrs. Jones for which he paid, at first, one pound a fortnight for their lodgings and he also was to provide extra money for food and milk.

Mr. and Mrs. Jones tried to extract more and more money from William Howells. As a result he was forced to move back into the lodgings as he could not afford to pay for his food and board and the children's elsewhere.

The pressure on William Howells must have been terribly hard and it was in October 1901 that the police were first called to 3 Rowley Terrace, where Inspector Jenkins found himself in a 'rough' house in the middle of a drunken row. Mrs Jones had accused William Howells of trying to kill his children. Mrs Jones said that Howells had told the older girl to throw the baby in the river and then to jump in herself. The girl naturally refused to carry out his request and he threatened to "knock her head off." As a result of the incident the police communicated with Inspector Thomas of the N.S.P.C.C. who called to the house himself on the 18th of October 1901. He found himself sickened by the unbelievable sight of

Elizabeth Ann, the youngest child. She was "reclining on an armchair in the kitchen with a crust of bread in her hand and was a mere skeleton, her eyes were sunken, she was totally blind, quite stiff and unable to move." The child was also unable to speak having been born mute. The father it seemed had been absent from the house for about a fortnight and Mrs Jones stated that she had no money to buy the child any milk.

At the trial Mr Howells said that he regularly gave the landlady money for the upkeep of his children but he believed that Mrs. Jones spent it on drink. Indeed, it seemed that Mrs. Jones was regularly seen to be drunk about the house and used the older child Mabel to fetch beer for her. Mr Howells and his landlady Mrs Jones were subsequently both charged with the neglect of the two children.

William received four months' hard labour and Rachel Jones had three months. The judge, a Mr. D. Thomas, summed up by saying that "The female defendant was not worthy of the name of woman, neither was Howells worthy of the name father."

Both children were taken to the workhouse where three year old Elizabeth was to die four months later. Despite being given nourishment there, her condition was so bad that when examined by Dr. Davies at the workhouse, he said "..... it presented a most pitiable, almost repulsive sight. The skin was practically lying on the bones and there was an entire absence of fat. It weighed 13Ibs and 3 oz instead of the expected 31Ibs. It was greatly emaciated and blind from want of nourishment, and unable to move its limbs owing to it being kept in a constrained position." When a post-mortem was carried out, it was found that the child had died due to chronic inflammation of the stomach. This was due to a long course of neglect and improper feeding. Mrs Jones, it transpired during the court case, had been feeding the child Bovril only.

At the Glamorgan assizes William Howells and Rachel Jones were charged on two indictments, one for feloniously killing and slaying Elizabeth Ann Howells on the 24th of February 1901, and on the coroner's inquisition for the manslaughter of the child.

It was a harrowing case of such a proportion that no words can describe the depths of despair and suffering that the children endured for the hopelessness of a father who in his own little way tried and a landlady who was driven by the greed she had for money and her liking for the drink.

PORTH BABY SCANDAL

A case that caused a sensation in Porth during February of 1905 began with the discovery of a new born baby's body in a garden. It was not so much the discovery of the baby, but the fact that its mother turned out to be thirteen years old.

Child mortality was high in the early part of the 1900s and although stillbirths were by law to be reported, many were not. The bodies were simply hidden, usually due to the mothers not wanting another mouth to feed, or the moral stigma attached to illegitimacy. As a result, due to lack of evidence, it was often never truly discovered whether the children were really stillborn or killed at birth.

The discovery of the baby's body was made by one Hannah Andrews of 12 Argyle street, Cymmer on Sunday the 5th of February 1905. She had gone down the garden on the Sunday morning at 11 o'clock and found the baby's body, which was naked, lying by the wall. It looked by its position as if it had been dropped over the wall from next door's garden, at number 11, rather than from the street.

Living at number 11 Argyle Street were a Mr and Mrs Valender and their orphaned grandchild Violet, who would be fourteen years old the following September.

An inquest was made into the discovery of the body to try and ascertain whether the baby was born alive or stillborn. The grandparents of Violet, when questioned, said that they had not noticed anything unusual about Violet's condition at that time as she had always been a 'robust' girl. On the Friday she had been attending to household duties and 7.30 the following morning her grandmother had left her in the kitchen drinking a cup of tea while she went out.

Whether Violet left the house at any time she did not know as the grandfather had been fast asleep in the kitchen. Dr. Cochrane who examined Violet on Sunday morning stated that, in his opinion, she had delivered a child about eighteen hours earlier. On examining the baby's body he considered that, as the lungs showed no evidence of having been inflated, the child must have been stillborn and had no "independent existence."

The coroner, Mr R.J. Rhys, in summing up to the jury said that the evidence all pointed to the fact that the child had been stillborn, but if it had drawn only one breath, 'The charge would be very grave indeed.As regards to the father of the child, he sincerely hoped that the man, whoever he might be, who was responsible for this would be found out. It did seem a monstrous thing that in a country like ours, a girl who would not be fourteen years of age until next September should be got into this condition. The man, if it could be brought home to him, deserved the severest punishment the law could inflict."

The man turned out to be a Mr. Percy Trewethy, a collier of Bedw Street, Cymmer, who was charged on the 23rd of February 1905, at Porth police court with 'carnally knowing' Violet Emily Valender between April and May 1904 Violet being at that time under the age of thirteen. But a remand was applied for and granted as Violet was still unable to attend. Percy was returned to Cardiff gaol to await the trial.

In the ensuing case, held in March, it was learnt that Mr. Trewethy was at the time lodging at the girl's house and had been for nearly two years. The grandfather and an uncle worked as colliery hauliers and did not return home from work until 8 p.m. and therefore the only people at home between 4 p.m. and 7p.m. were Violet, her grandmother and Percy. Violet and Percy were often left alone together in the kitchen and it was here that the alleged assault took place, not once but over a few weeks numerous times. Violet stated that when it happened the first time she had screamed out, but her grandmother who was upstairs on all occasions denied hearing anything.

Percy also denied the charge only stating that he and Violet often "larked about" but that nothing immoral had ever taken place.

The commissioner, a Mr. Harrison Q.C. who heard the case decided that the evidence of the girl was unsatisfactory as if, as she alleged, the affairs had taken place over a number of weeks, then surely her grandmother would have heard something. In summing up he was to comment on, "..... the danger of finding a verdict of guilty on the uncorroborated statement of a young child."

The verdict of 'not guilty' on Percy Trewethy was followed by applause from the back of the court, but this was immediately suppressed.

If the case had arisen today in the 2000s, the outcome might have been different due to the discovery in 1984 of DNA profiling. A child inherits half the chromosomes from each of its parents and a simple test could easily have determined whether Percy Trewethy was indeed the natural father of the dead child.

TREHERBERT BABY SCANDAL

A sad but strange case came to light during the evening of Tuesday the 5th of May 1908, concerning the discovery of a murdered baby on a train.

A young collier, Gwilym Jones Humphreys, had been drinking all day at The Greyhound pub in Pontypridd with his friend Thomas May from Ynysybwl. At 10.15 p.m., Gwilym boarded the train alone at Pontypridd intending to get off at Treorchy and then walk up Cwmparc to Park Road where he lived. He was alone in the railway carriage and when he sat down he noticed a parcel under the seat. However after drinking in the pub all day long, Gwilym fell asleep and went past his destination of Treorchy station and woke up when the train reached Treherbert.

Gwilym decided to pick up the parcel and disembark. The porter at Treherbert station noticed Gwilym had a parcel under his arm, when he asked him for his ticket the porter also noticed a peculiar smell emanating from the parcel.

In the darkness of the evening Gwilym Humphreys also became aware of the awful smell that came from the parcel he had picked up, he also noticed that it was soft to the touch. Not wishing to examine its contents, Gwilym quickly threw the parcel down into a lane that led into the Treherbert football field, near to some stables.

The following morning a baby's body, wrapped up in paper and linen with its feet exposed, was the gory sight that greeted John Williams, a brake driver, who discovered the parcel.

Dr. D. Charles Williams received the body on the same day and conducted a post-mortem. At the inquest on the following Friday, the doctor caused a sensation when he expressed the opinion that the child had been born alive but had been murdered. It had been smothered by something being placed over its mouth, as the nose was twisted to one side.

The unfortunate Gwilym Humphreys, having been witnessed in possession of the parcel, was duly arrested late on the Friday morning and charged with "Concealing the birth of a newly born male infant child." Luckily for Gwilym his friend Thomas May attested that he had no parcel with him when he boarded the train at Pontypridd. Also Dr. Williams confirmed that the child had probably been dead for seven to nine days.

Gwilym Humphreys had by now probably been wishing that he had never laid eyes on the parcel in the first place. The coroner in addressing Humphreys stated that ".......he had evidently acted on the principle that findings were keepings, but noticing that the parcel smelt very badly, which could not be the case with a suit of clothes........he threw it away. It would have been his duty to hand over the parcel to a railway official.....You have only yourself to thank for it and it just serves you right."

Gwilym Humphreys was duly dismissed with a warning from the judge who told him "You are a very foolish fellow, and I don't suppose that you would have got into this trouble if you were not drunk. Let this be a warning to you to keep off the drink."

The verdict on the case was one of "wilful murder against some person or persons unknown."

No trace of the parentage of the child was ever obtained and sadly the identity of the child remains to this day unknown.

YSTRAD'S BABY IN THE DRAINPIPE

A mysterious incident that caused a sensation was that of the "baby's body in the drainpipe", in March of 1916. The crime of 'concealing a birth', was not uncommon and meant that the bodies of babies were found in all manner of odd places.

It must have come though as a severe shock to Councillor Thomas James when, in the course of investigating a blocked drain at the back of his house at 50 Penrhys Road, he discovered that the blockage was the head of a child which had been severed from its body. The police were summoned and it was P.C. Stonehouse who made the further grim discovery of the child's body in the main drain, the arms were never found.

Doctors W.E. Thomas and Quigley did a post-mortem on the body and were in agreement that the child "Had had a separate existence", as it had been born alive. The doctors also concluded that the baby had been dead for about one to two days.

At the inquest, held by Mr R.J. Rhys coroner, there was little other evidence on which to build a case, so in summing up he said the jury had only the one decision to make, whether it was a case of murder or the minor crime of a concealment of birth. In his opinion murder was not an option as there would seem little reason to sever the head and arms. It seemed simply a case of the child dying through lack of attention at birth, it's body being mutilated to aid the concealment. It did not take long for the jury to reach an 'open verdict' and the case was closed. The parents were never traced.

Although the case was reported as the 'Ystrad Sensation', in comparison with today's standards and attitudes, the case would have caused a much greater sensation. Far more time and effort would have been spent on an investigation by the police into the whereabouts of the parents of the dead child. It seems then as if it was just another case of the discovery of the body of an unwanted, illegitimate working class child, one of many who would forever remain anonymous and just become another grim statistic on the files of the authorities.

Today in the twenty first century, this lack of interest among the middle class authorities seems to be astounding. Then, in the early part of the 20th century, it was just another part of the reality of working-class life.

A CASE OF INSANITY IN PONTYPRIDD 1943

At 9.20 a.m. on October 25th 1943, Doctor Gwyn H. Evans arrived at the home of John Martin aged 43 and his sister Gertrude Martin age 63, who resided at 42 Hopkinstown Road Pontypridd. The Doctor arrived at the request of a P.C. Evans who had arrived at the house a short while earlier after being called by a neighbour of the Martin's.

In the front room on the ground floor of the house, Doctor Evans saw John and his sister Gertrude lying together on a bed. Blood stained the bedclothing and both John and Gertrude had their throats wrapped up.

Doctor Evans first inspected Gertrude, discovering that she had a wound on the left hand side of her neck. Because the wound was not bleeding, Doctor Evans replaced Gertrude's dressing.

Gertrude Martin was incoherent with her speech and was making noises, she would not, or could not answer any of the Doctor's questions as to how she had sustained her injury.

John Martin however, declared to the Doctor that he had suffered a bad night. He had, he stated got up at 6 a.m. and gone into the other room to light a fire. Whilst he was in the other room, he had, he stated seen a knife on the table, he felt when seeing the knife that using it would offer an easy way out. Picking up the knife he returned to where his sister was in the other room and cut her throat with it. Upon hearing these facts, Doctor Evans immediately arranged for John and his sister Gertrude to be removed to the Central Homes.

Later that day Doctor Arthur Jenkins visited Central Homes in order to examine Gertrude Martin. He found her to be in a miserable state. She was suffering from shock and muttering incoherently. Gertrude seemed unable to answer any questions that were put to her by the Doctor.

The wound in Gertrude's throat was bad enough to require Doctor Jenkins to insert fourteen stitches into it. Despite being placed under medical care, Gertrude Martin died at 4.10 a.m. the following morning.

John Martin had five stitches inserted into his self inflicted throat wound. His physical condition was considered to be quite good, despite his wound. When asked why he had done such a thing, Martin again replied that he thought that it was the only way out.

Gertrude Martin's body was removed to Cardiff, where Doctor Gough, pathologist performed a post - mortem. He found the wound in Gertrude Martin's neck to be seven and a half inches long, at which he felt was a homicidal wound. Gertrude also had chronic T.B. The cause of her death was shock and haemorrhage due to a cut throat. Her body through disease was wasted and may have been contributory in enhancing her death.

John Martin was, following his sister's death, visited at the Central Homes by P.C. Gomer Evans on the 2nd November to inform him that he was to be taken to Pontypridd Police station, where he would be charged with the murder of his sister.

On Tuesday 16th November, John Martin found himself in the dock to answer for a crime he freely cared to admit. As a result he as committed to take trial at the next Assizes.

On December 9th 1943, at the trial, it was stated that John Martin was suffering from depression and melancholia. He felt that he should kill his sister and himself in order not be a burden to society. It was further disclosed that in October John Martin's brother had committed suicide by hanging himself.

Gertrude Martin, it was stated, had been in poor health for quite some time, this caused something of a burden to John Martin, who by accounts, had trouble coping with the situation. John Martin denied malice in committing his crime and apparently did not appreciate the true seriousness of his crime. It was concluded that John Martin did not know he was doing anything wrong.

As a result of this conclusion, John Martin was found guilty of murder, but was declared to be totally insane. Mr. Justice Lawrence ordered that

John Martin be detained at His Majesty's pleasure.

TREHERBERT INFANTICIDE

A lot of mothers could easily sympathise and be able to identify with the following case and the sad circumstances that surrounded the Treherbert woman who was involved in the case during June of 1945.

The woman involved was a Mrs Irene Vaughan of Ynyswen Road in Treherbert. She was the young wife of a soldier who had been serving in the army for five years and, as a result of the Second World War, had spent much of his time away. She had three children, a nine year old, a five year old and a four and a half month old baby girl called Christine. For the two years prior to 1945, Mrs Vaughan had been seeing her G.P., a Dr. Morris, because of her nerves.

The doctor in a statement that he later made at court, confirmed that he had been treating Mrs Vaughan for "nervous debility", for some time. He considered that her state of anxiety had been of such concern that he had given her a certificate recommending that her husband be granted special leave from the army in order to return home to support her. Since the birth of her third child Christine, he thought that what he termed her "melancholia" had greatly increased.

Otherwise he considered her to be a good mother and very devoted to her children. But the doctor's certificate of recommendation was not dealt with quickly enough to bring Mr Vaughan home in time to prevent the tragic events that took place on the early morning of the 19th of June 1945. The baby Christine, had been a difficult child since birth and was accustomed to spend most of her time crying through the night. Mrs Vaughan, already trying to cope with the upbringing of her other two children on her own most of the time and already suffering with her depression finally reached her breaking point on the morning of the 19th of June.

For the previous two nights she had gained very little sleep, Christine keeping her up with her crying. On the eve of June the 19th, after having put the other two children to bed she spent the rest of the night trying to calm Christine and get her to sleep. In her own statement, made later to the police, Mrs Vaughan was to say, "I tried picking her up and putting her in with me, I tried everything to get her quiet, but it was of no use."

How many women have reached that point where, through lack of sleep and in desperation, they have wished their child dead? But Mrs Vaughn, probably not realising the gravity of what she was doing, put those thoughts into action and taking a silk stocking wrapped it around the neck of Christine and proceeded to strangle her. "She just screamed a bit and then she was quiet." Mrs. Vaughan later stated.

It is hard to imagine the exact thoughts that must have gone through Mrs Vaughan's mind as the extent of what she had done hit her. The relief that the crying had stopped must soon have been overtaken by horror as she looked down at her daughter, now lying dead in her cot with the silk stocking around her neck. Mrs Vaughan, in some shock, took herself downstairs and sat in a chair through the dark early hours before dawn, wondering how she would be able to act normally enough to get her other two children up and off to school. Somehow she managed to do so and afterwards went straight to the police station where she was to confess to Inspector Evans what she had done. The Inspector went to the house and found Christine lying dead in the cot, the stocking still around her neck, just as Mrs Vaughan had left her.

It clearly was a case of what would be termed today 'post natal depression' taken to the extreme. Realising what she had done and feeling the full force of guilt and remorse for her actions, Mrs. Vaughan did not attempt to hide the facts in an endeavour to cover up her guilt.

She confessed fully to what she had done and as a result was charged with the murder of her baby daughter.

However in the ensuing case, the statements given by Dr. Morris regarding her devotion to her children and also the testaments of several neighbours, who stated that she was a woman with a 'high moral character' and a wonderful mother, helped to gain her some sympathy at court and caused Mr Richard John, the county prosecuting solicitor, to address the bench and request "That Mrs Vaughan should be committed to the assizes not on a charge of murder, but on the lesser charge of infanticide." It was clear he said, "That at the time the accused was alleged to have caused the death of her child, she had not fully recovered from giving birth to it and the balance of her mind was disturbed." Mrs Vaughan, at her trial sat with a bowed head and wept quietly ...... a tragic figure, as she stood, her uniformed husband at her side to hear the sentence passed.

The counsel in an outburst of sudden eloquenc, quoted the theme of Robert Bridges, poet laureate, that "Life was balanced on a razor edge."

They asked the judge to deal with the accused as sympathetically as he could. Mrs Vaughan was bound over for twelve months on her undertaking to reside at an institution recommended by the probation officer, where she could be properly looked after.

PENTRE CHILD MURDER 1949

How the overpowering and misdirected love of a mother could have ended up in the death of her only child is the question raised by the tragic murder of thirteen year old Valerie Linda Williams by her mother, forty-six year old Linda Violet Williams on 29th April 1949 at their home in Baglan Street, Pentre.

Valerie had been described as being a tall attractive fair haired child, who attended Bronllwyn school in Gelli. She was very popular with her many school friends and had a quiet and pleasant disposition, she was unobtrusive and inoffensive. Valerie lived with her widowed mother Mrs Linda Williams, her father having died in August 1944. Another woman, a Mrs Maud Graff had also been living with the mother and daughter, probably as a paying lodger, for the last three and a half years.

On Saturday the 29th of April, Mrs Graff (in her statement,) said she could remember Valerie coming home from school and proudly showing her mother a letter she had written to send to relatives in Australia. Earlier that morning, according to Mrs Graff, Mrs Williams had asked her if she could borrow a hammer and a sweeping brush. Later Mrs Graff heard the noise of hammering coming from Mrs Williams's bedroom, but she thought little of it at the time. Much later that night, at about 11.45 p.m., Mrs Graff said that she retired to bed, her bedroom being next door to Mrs Williams's, which she shared with Valerie. The next that Mrs Graff knew was that she was woken in the early hours by the sounds of moaning and groaning, but they appeared to come from outside, so she thought little of the noise and went back to sleep.

At 7.45 a.m. Mrs Graff got up and went downstairs to make herself a cup of tea and also one for Mrs. Williams, but when she brought the tea upstairs Mrs Graff found that the bedroom door was, unusually, locked. Mrs Graff knocked on the bedroom door and called out to Mrs Williams, who answered in a hoarse voice. "Who is it, what do you want?" She also refused the tea. Mrs Graff became very concerned at the strange behaviour

The grave site of Valerie Linda Williams? Treorchy Cemetery

of Linda Williams. As a result of her concern, she went for assistance to Mrs Williams's sister's house.

Upon returning to the house they found Mrs Williams coming downstairs. She was half dressed and clearly very upset. Linda Williams sat down at the kitchen table and told the two women present that Valerie was dead upstairs in the bedroom.

When the police inspector and the doctor were called they found Valerie as her mother had said, upstairs on the bed, looking as if she was asleep but she was clearly dead. There were no signs of violence inflicted upon the girl however there was a strong smell of gas in the bedroom. A quilt was left half draped over the window with another quilt nailed over the mantelpiece and held down with bricks in the grate. When this was removed, there was found to be a pillow stuffed up the chimney piece. There was a gas bracket on the wall from which had been removed the burner and mantle and a length of tubing was found on the floor together with some sleeping pills. As a result of these findings Mrs Linda Violet Williams was charged with the murder of her daughter Valerie Linda Williams by carbon monoxide poisoning.

It is perhaps difficult to understand why a woman, who it was said was a very devoted mother, who worshiped her daughter more than anything else and would deprive herself and her home to provide for Valerie, yet could have taken her young life away.

But at the ensuing trial the reasons became clearer as it was revealed that since her husband's death Mrs Williams had suffered a nervous breakdown and, although she had tried to provide a normal life for herself and Valerie, she had found it increasingly difficult to live with her nerves and decided that the only way out was to kill herself. However, the one thing she worried about more than anything else was that Valerie would be left alone with no-one to care for her. Also she did not want her only child to have to live through the rest of her life as the object of gossip and pity. There were also her fears that Valerie would end up suffering with her nerves. So rather than let her daughter not only suffer as she had done, but suffer alone, she decided to end bothof their lives as quickly and painlessly as she could, through gas poisoning. To this end she had first given Valerie sleeping tablets so that she would fall quietly asleep, ignorant that it would be her last as her mother blocked up the window and the chimney and turned on the gas, which she hoped would end both of their lives.

Tragically for Linda Williams her plans went wrong, her beloved daughter had died while she remained alive to face the bitter consequences. Two letters that she had written and left on the mantelpiece in the bedroom were read out in court and both in their poignancy show her deep feelings and concern she felt for Valerie. The first letter was for her sister, and read "I cannot carry on any longer, I have tried to fight my nerves. I did not know what I was doing only I never told anyone for fear they would send me down there. Life is not worth living when like this everyday. I have ruined Valerie's nerves and I am afraid if I leave her she will end up down there. So I am taking her with me, because people would only point her out and her life would not be worth living. So we are going to Will (her husband) and won't worry anyone. I know that God will forgive me because he knows how hard I have tried to come better. I hope that God will never give you a nervous breakdown. Goodbye everybody. Bury us with Will. Now I know we are at rest, Valerie and Violet. My insurances will bury us."

The second letter written by Linda Williams was written to a friend, a Mrs Tegan of Avondale Road in Gelli. It read, "Forgive me for what I have done. I cannot carry on and I want to thank you for your kindness. Goodbye my dear and look after yourself. I cannot leave Valerie. I love her too much."

Linda Violet Williams was found guilty of her daughter's murder, but was considered insane at the criminal court. One can only feel sympathy for a woman who, having suffered before, now faced the rest of her life alone and guiltridden with a penance that would never be paid.

Poor Valerie's funeral, which took place on the 5th of May 1949, was attended by hundreds of sympathisers who had gathered in Pentre to watch, as silently the funeral cortege left her uncle's house in Treharne Street. The road was lined with people who came from near and afar, many were women with babes in their arms. Valerie was taken to Treorchy cemetery where she was buried, the Rev. Glenville Jones of Monah Chapel officiating.

YNYSHIR INFANTICIDE

A sad case of infanticide occurred in Ynyshir in March 1955. All murder cases involving children are to say the least difficult to understand but this one particularly so, especially as it appeared to the police and everyone else involved in the case as a 'completely motiveless murder'. Michael Thomas Jones, the victim, had been a happy twelve month old 'Bonny golden haired child.' He was the youngest of four children who lived with their parents, Mr and Mrs Emrys Jones and his paternal grandparents Mr and Mrs Thomas Jones at 16, Whitting Street, Ynyshir.

Early on the morning of the 28th of March 1955, Mrs Edith Jones remembered seeing her son Emrys carry the baby Michael downstairs. Michael had been crying . Mrs Jones left them together in the sitting room for two minutes and Emrys began to boil up some milk for the baby.

When Mrs Jones returned to the sitting room, she was quite unprepared for the horrific sight that met her eyes. Emrys was just sitting there looking very agitated, but when Mrs Jones asked him what the matter was, he did not reply. Then looking down at the floor, she saw the body of Michael.

The reports in the papers in those earlier days were much more graphic with details of murders and the local paper described the scene as where, "The walls of the living room were splattered with blood to the height of 6ft 4 ins, in one place. There was a pool of blood under the dead baby's head and a poker lying close by bore blood stains at the handle end." Michael had died of a fractured skull, laceration of the brain and multiple injuries of the head.

The murder baffled everyone as the reasons for such a horrific killing appeared to be motiveless.

For a father who had been described as being, "A good affectionate father, particularly affectionate towards baby Michael", to have suddenly turned and battered his son to death with a poker was beyond comprehension. It was a crime that he freely admitted to. In his own words to the police Emrys said, "I put the baby down on the floor, and I picked up the poker and hit him on the head with it. I hit him a couple of times. My mother came in and I told her that I had killed the baby."

It seems clear that Emrys did not fully realise what he was doing at the time and it emerged during the course of the investigation that he had been suffering for some time from mental depression and severe headaches. He had in fact a long history of mental problems, which had caused him to be discharged from the army. His medical record at the time stated that he had, "Recovered from his depressive phase following a course of electro-convulsion therapy, but remains a mentally unstable individual, lacking in self-confidence and easily disheartened."

These depressive states continued after he left the mental hospital at Bridgend, where he had been admitted in February 1955, and he remained with feelings of unworthiness, feeling that he had let his wife and family down, due to his inability to work. Life in fact, to Emrys, was not worth living. Dr. Fenton who examined Emrys, felt that he was clearly suffering from depressive insanity. A symptom of this disease was that the patient felt he had brought ruination upon those near and dear to him.

In addressing the jury of twelve men, Edmund Davies Q.C. showed much sympathy to Emrys when he said that, "This man, at the time of his action, was insane within the definition of our law. He was a loving father. This is not a case where the defendant was shown to be a cruel tyrant, hot-headed and ill-tempered. He is a good and loving father who has found the stress of life too much for his mental state. Fear seemed to have been Jones's inheritance. He feared everything. He feared the army service, feared people, feared his work, feared unemployment, feared that he was not doing enough for his family - fears of that kind piled up all on top of one another until he killed his child, in regard of whom, he was described as being a loving father."

The jury conferred without leaving the box and took only one minute to reach a verdict of, "Guilty but insane." Emrys Thomas Jones was ordered to be kept in strict custody at Broadmoor, until Her Majesty's pleasure be known.

Maybe if Emrys had received the help he clearly needed in time, such a tragic event would never have happened.

So ends another sad and tragic case, one of so many that littered the history of our dark past.